Published in Great Britain by **Cassell Publishers Limited**
Villiers House, 41/47 Strand, London WC2N 5JE

Published in the United States of America by **Liturgical Press**
St John's Abbey, Collegeville, Minnesota 56321

English text © Cassell Publishers Limited 1991
French text © Editions du Centurion 1989
Illustrations © PROCIDA 1983.

Adapted from *Granracconto* by Marino Nicora and Vittorino Joannes
Original edition first published by Editions du Centurion, Paris 1989
English-language edition first published 1991

British Library Cataloguing-in-Publication Data can be obtained on request from the British Library.

ISBN 0 304 32325 X (Cassell)
      0-8146-2064-7 (Liturgical Press)

Typeset by Chapterhouse, The Cloisters, Halsall Lane, Formby, Merseyside
Printed and bound in France by Bayard Presse

TELL ME
THE BIBLE

Words: Joëlle Chabert and François Mourvillier

Pictures: Letizia Galli

From the "GRANRACCONTO", by Vittorino Joannes and Marino Nicora,
a television programme produced by PROCIDA

CASSELL

THE LITURGICAL PRESS
Collegeville, Minnesota

I'm going to tell you stories, and you can tell them to other people later on

I can't tell you the whole Bible of course. I'm going to choose good stories, which are easier to tell than teaching or proverbs or even prayers.

Storytelling means adding a bit here and there, mixing every day language with poetry and the words of a prophet. As you tell stories you see new things in them ...

When I tell you the Bible stories I'm like all the people down hundreds and thousands of years, passing the stories from person to person.

Imagine: more than three thousand years ago men and women heard from their mothers and fathers, the adventures of their ancestors, the Hebrew nomads God chose to show that God is with us human beings.

They must have really tried to remember every word passed on by their ancestors; every word was a treasure. Perhaps they had actions and rhythms which helped them to remember the words. Maybe some of the stories got lost. Others maybe were told in different styles in different places, in the north or the south.

Later, from about a thousand years before Jesus was born, people started to write down the stories collected over the generations. It wasn't always easy to put the bits together. Just to get the first five books of the Bible together from five different traditions took five hundred years.

The Bible is really a library, full of story books. And they are all needed to tell the story of God and the Hebrews – now we call them the Jews – the story of their friendship and their promises to each other. We call these promises the Covenant, because they tell us about the Covenant between God and all the peoples of the world.

Testament is an old word for Covenant or Promise. Christians call the two parts of the Bible the Old Testament and the New Testament and you will see these two parts in *Tell me the Bible*. The Old Testament is the Bible of the Jews.

Look hard at the pictures. They will stay in your memory. Listen to the stories. They have been built up over the centuries like the place where you live. But remember: the words don't say everything. The meaning can be hidden in the silences, and in what the words don't say.

Imagine yourself in the stories of Eve, Jacob, Moses, David, Jonah, Zacchaeus, Martha and Paul. Suddenly you'll think, 'That's like me. That's like the story of my life.'

The Bible comes from long ago, and it will go on far into the future. I'm going to tell it to you, and you can tell other people later on...

First story of creation

**First, the Bible tells of
the Creation as the beginning
of the world, and the beginning of
all life on earth,
now and in the past.**

When God created the sky and the earth, everything was shapeless and empty. Everything was in deep darkness.

The spirit of God moved over the chaos. The spirit of God wandered over the surface of the waters.

And God said 'Let there be light.' And there was light. And God saw that the light was good and God separated the light from the darkness. And God called the light 'day' and the darkness 'night'.

God said, 'Let there be a space to divide above from below.' And it was so. God called the space 'sky'.

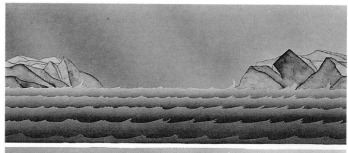

In the sixth century before the birth of Jesus a lot of Jews were in exile far from their country, and they were in despair. Those who had faith wrote down this story to show that God wanted a happy life for everyone.

God said, 'Let the waters below the sky come together and let the dry part appear.' And it was so. God called the dry part 'land' and he called the collected waters 'sea'. And God saw that it was good.

God said, 'Let the land be covered with green, with plants and their seeds and fruit trees.' It was so, and God saw that it was good.

God said, 'Let there be lights in the sky to separate day from night, to mark the times and the seasons.' God saw that this was good.

God said, 'Let the waters bring forth fish, and let birds fly in the sky.' God saw that this was good. He blessed them: 'Multiply yourselves, fill the seas and the sky in millions.'

God said, 'Let the earth produce living creatures, cattle and creeping things.' And it was so. God saw that this was good.

God said, 'Let us make humans in our image, and likeness.' God created human beings in God's image; man and woman were created. God blessed them and said, 'Be fruitful and multiply, fill the earth and care for it. I am giving you the earth and all its seeds and all its fruits.' God saw all that had been made and it was very good.

Thus the man and the woman were given the job of making a happy world and passing on life, in the image of God.

Second story of creation

**This story is often called
'The Story of Original Sin' because it
tells us how everything went wrong
because Adam and Eve wanted
to be all-powerful and to take the
place of God: and this is
true of everyone.**

each animal a name. But none of them was a true companion. So God put Adam into a deep sleep, took one of his ribs and made it into a woman.

When Adam woke up he was amazed. 'This is my other half,' he said. 'We will live side by side.' Adam called her 'Eve' which means 'full of life'. They looked at each other face to face, and loved each other. But the crafty serpent approached Eve and said, 'The Lord God has told you not to touch the Tree of the Knowledge of Good and Evil or you will die. But you won't die. You will know everything, and you will be like God. God is afraid that you will make yourselves into gods.'

Eve saw that this tree was beautiful, precious and good. She picked a fruit and she and Adam ate it.

God made the man from the earth, and breathed into his nostrils the breath of life; the man became a living being. This was 'Adam', which means 'the earthman' and God put him in a garden. In the middle of the garden, there was the Tree of Life and the Tree of the Knowledge of Good and Evil.

God said, 'It is not good that the man should be alone. He needs someone to keep him company.' So God gave Adam the animals and Adam gave

thought they could be gods. Now they will have no more chance to pick the fruit of the Tree of Life.' And the Lord God drove Adam and Eve out of the garden.

Everything became clear. Adam and Eve were not as foolish as the animals. Their eyes were opened and they saw that they were naked and had no defences. They were embarrassed and wanted to make themselves clothes of fig leaves. Then they heard the footsteps of God, who was walking in the cool of the evening. They ran to hide. But God called them, 'Why are you hiding? You've eaten the forbidden fruit.' They were frightened. Adam said it was Eve's fault and Eve said it was the serpent's fault.

The Lord God rebuked the serpent, 'You will slither on your stomach, and you will eat dust for the rest of your life.' Then God told Adam and Eve, 'You will have to struggle to cultivate the land: thorns will grow and brambles will flourish. You will earn your living by the sweat of your brow, and then you will die. Dust you are, and unto dust you shall return.'

The Lord God made clothes of animal skin for Adam and Eve, and said, 'Man and woman wanted to be equal to me, so they ate the fruit of the Tree of the Knowledge of Good and Evil. They

Time passed. Adam and Eve had two sons: Cain, who became a farmer, and Abel, who became a shepherd. At harvest time, to thank God, Cain offered up some of his crops from his fields. Abel offered up a lamb from his flocks. Cain thought that God accepted Abel's sacrifice but rejected his own. He was offended and his anger grew fierce, like a wounded lion, ready to pounce: he attacked Abel and killed him.

The Lord said to Cain, 'Where is your brother?' And Cain replied, 'Am I my brother's keeper?' So God cursed Cain, 'From now on you are a lost soul, and you will search for your way for ever.' And Cain went away, heavy-hearted.

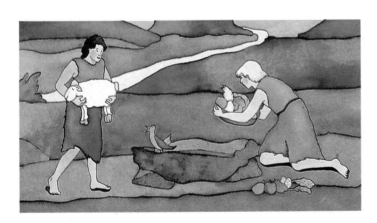

The flood

**However much people dream
of paradise, they cannot
hide wickedness.
Why doesn't God get rid
of wicked people?**

The inhabitants of the earth had started to grow in number. The Lord God saw that wickeness was growing too, to the point where God regretted creating people. God swore to wipe them from the face of the earth, and drown them all in the sea.

There was only one just person in God's eyes: Noah. God said to him, 'The world is full of violence because of human beings. I am going to destroy them. I shall destroy all that I have created.'

But God added, 'Noah, make a huge ship of wood and reeds, 300 cubits long, 50 cubits wide and three storeys high. Cover it with tar and put a pointed roof on it and cut a door in the side of it. It will be called an ark.

Then get into the ark with your wife, your three sons and their wives, because you are the only just person I can find. Take a male and a female from every species of animal, and a supply of food. I am going to send a flood. I shall make it rain on the earth, and everything on earth will die.'

Noah obeyed God. He embarked on the ark with his family and two of every animal of every species.

The flood came. Flood waters swelled the rivers to overflowing. Everything was swallowed up by the waters, even the mountains. Birds, animals, insects, women, men, children, and all who lived on the earth died.

The only creatures left alive were Noah and those who were with him in the ark.

Then God remembered Noah, and sent a wind to earth and the rains stopped and the waters started to go down. Forty days later, Noah opened the window of the ark and sent out a crow, then a dove, to see if the water had gone down. But they

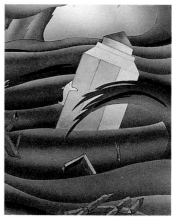

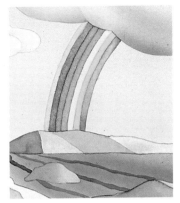

found no dry place to perch and so they came back to the ark. Seven days passed. Noah sent the dove out again, and she came back with an olive branch in her beak.

So the waters had gone down, and plants were starting to grow again.

Seven days later, Noah sent out the dove again, and she did not return. This time the waters had really gone down. The ark had come to rest on the highest mountain in the known world. Noah lifted the roof of the ark and saw dry land and, on the horizon, a huge rainbow which joined the earth to the sky.

Soon after, Noah got everyone out of the ark. Then he offered to God the best fruits of the new world.

Then God made a promise, 'I shall never again curse the earth, I shall never again destroy the earth, even when human beings are wicked. As long as the earth shall endure, seed time and harvest, summer and winter, day and night, will never cease.'

God blessed Noah, 'I am making a covenant for ever with all living creatures, with you, your children and your children's children. Here is the sign of our covenant: the rainbow which joins the earth and sky.'

The Tower of Babel

This is a story to explain
why different peoples do not
understand each other, and
why nations want to
conquer the world.

In those days all the people of the earth spoke the same language, and all used the same words.

People moved around with their flocks. Towards the east they found a great plain to settle down in. They said to each other, 'Let's make bricks with clay and straw and water, let's shape them and bake them and build walls with them.'

And they built walls.

The bricks took the place of the stones, because there weren't many stones in that area, and they used bitumen to cement them together.

They said to each other, 'Let's build a city, and let's make a tower which reaches right up to the sky. That will make us famous; we'll make a name for ourselves and we'll be world-famous. We'll be the greatest in the world. No-one will be able to compete with us.'

Were they trying to reach as high as God? Always higher and higher, the tower was built.

They were so carried away with their ambition, they built a giant tower reaching right up to the sky. You might have called it a spear to pierce the clouds, or a huge door to get into heaven.

So the Lord came to see the city and the tower, and maybe was impressed by the mighty power of human beings when they decide to work together.

God said, 'They think they are all-powerful. I shall muddle up their speech and throw their language into confusion. They will not be able to understand each other any more.'

The Lord confused their language. They all started to talk in different languages and they could not understand anything each other said.

What a terrible confusion.

It led to quarrels, they got into arguments, and lost all trust in one another.

They stopped building the city. Its name was Babel, which means 'confusion'. Then the Lord God drove its inhabitants away to every part of the earth.

———

That is the end of this giddy story, where God seemed to think that human beings were getting above themselves.

That is the end of this story told by people who guessed that real greatness doesn't necessarily mean being higher up than other people.

God's promise

More than 3000 years
ago people were already telling
the stories about Abraham.
They tell us about a God who
wants to live among people, and a
person who lived in the
presence of God.

Abraham was seventy-five. He left his country
and set off with his wife Sara, his nephew Lot, his
servants and his animals and all his possessions.
They all set off for the land of Canaan.

In those days a tribe of nomads settled near the
village of Haran. Its chief was called Abraham,
son of Terah. Abraham had a nephew, Lot, and a
wife, Sara, but no children. Sara could not have
children.

Abraham heard a call from the Lord God, 'Leave
your father's house, and go towards the country I
will show you. I will make you the father of a
great nation and I will bless you. I will make your
name great. And in you all the families of the
earth will be blessed.'

Lot chose the Jordan valley, a ribbon of green between the dry brown hills, a real paradise. He went off to settle near Sodom, a town where people did not know the Lord God.

Abraham stayed in the mountains of Canaan.

After this parting, the Lord God spoke again to Abraham, 'Fear nothing, Abraham; I am your shield and I will keep you safe.' Abraham prayed to God, 'Lord, I'm old already, I'm going to die,

They arrived at the oak of Moreh, at Sichem. God met Abraham there and made him this promise, 'I will give this country to your descendants.'

Abraham and those who were with him set up an altar so that people would always remember that this country was given to them by God.

Then they continued their journey south.

Abraham was very rich in gold and in flocks. Lot, his nephew, who was with him, also had flocks. And there was not enough land to feed their animals. So an argument broke out between their shepherds. So Abraham said to Lot, 'I don't want arguments between us, because we are like brothers. It's a big country. Let's separate; you choose where you want to go.'

and I've no children to leave behind me.' Then God said, 'Look at the sky. Can you count the stars? You will have as many descendants as the stars in the sky.'

Abraham began to trust again in the promise of God. He put himself in God's hands, and God saw his faith.

The mysterious visit

**Abraham was
counting on God's promise,
but it still didn't come true.
How could he go
on trusting?**

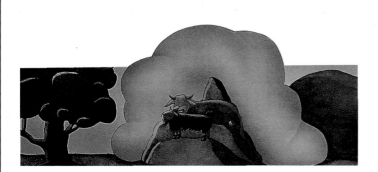

The years passed. But there was still a great emptiness in the life of Abraham and his wife Sara: they had no children to bring up. Sara could not have children. For her it was like an evil spell. One day she said to Abraham, 'I can't have children. So according to the custom here I'm giving you my maid, Hagar. If you like, she will have a baby for you instead of me.'

One day Abraham heard a call, 'I am the Lord who led you from your fathers' country to give you this country. Prepare a young cow, a goat, a ram and a turtle dove.' Abraham obeyed, but he didn't know what was happening to him, as if he was lost in the dark. What was going to happen to him? Could he go on blindly trusting in God? In the darkness a flame flitted over the animals he had prepared. It was God passing over them, and God was renewing the promise and promising to keep it: Abraham would have descendants and a country.

Once she was pregnant, Hagar refused to go on being a servant, and looked down on Sara. Sara got angry with Abraham: 'It's your fault,' she said. Abraham replied, 'Do what you want with her.'

Sara was so cruel to Hagar that she ran away, towards Egypt, her own country.

In the desert, she heard a message from God, 'You will have a baby boy, and you will call him Ishmael, which means "God hears", because God has heard your grief.' Hagar had faith in God, and her son was born.

Soon afterwards, Abraham settled at Mamre. It was high noon, and Abraham was having a siesta at the door of his tent. That was where God appeared to him. He saw three strangers and ran to meet them, bowed before them and invited them to stay with him, 'My Lord, do me the honour of stopping here. There's water to refresh you and to wash your feet. Rest under this oak. I will get you some food.'

He rushed towards the flock and chose a tender calf and had it cooked. Then he asked Sara, 'Make three of those cakes you do so well.' Abraham brought the visitors the grilled meat, yoghurt and milk. He served the visitors and stayed standing nearby while they ate.

One of the guests asked Abraham, 'Where is your wife?' And he replied, 'There, in her tent.' The visitor said, 'I'll be back this way next year, and Sara will have a son.'

Abraham wondered who this traveller was, who repeated the promise of God. Could it actually be God?

Sara had heard everything, and she burst out laughing, 'I can't have children at my age. And Abraham is an old man too.' The Lord said to Abraham, 'Why is Sara laughing like that? Is there anything God can't do?' Then the visitors went off towards Sodom, the town at the bottom of the valley.

The lesson of Sodom

In those days there was
an earthquake.
In the Bible story this was
a punishment for
the people of Sodom
who had no respect for life.

The Lord said, 'If I find ten just people in Sodom I shall not destroy the city.'
  The Lord went away, and Abraham, like a true believer, trusted in God.

God did not keep any secrets from Abraham, and told him, 'The people of Sodom have no respect for life.' Abraham suspected Sodom was in danger, and started to beg the Lord, 'Are you going to punish the innocent people with the guilty ones? There could be as many as fifty good people in that town.' The Lord said, 'If I find fifty just people in Sodom I will spare the whole city.' Abraham got bolder, 'I am only dust,' he said, 'but listen all the same. Supposing there were five less than fifty.' The Lord said, 'If I find forty-five just people in Sodom I shall not destroy it.'

  Abraham went on, 'Perhaps there are only forty.' God said, 'For forty, I shall not punish it.' Abraham said, 'Don't get annoyed with me, but what if there are only thirty?' The Lord said, 'I shall not punish it if there are thirty.' Abraham went on, 'If I dared, I would say twenty'. The Lord said, 'All right, twenty then.' Abraham went on bargaining, 'Excuse me, but what about ten?'

Two messengers of God arrived at Sodom. Abraham's nephew Lot invited them to stay the night. They were having dinner when the local people surrounded the house shouting, 'Down with foreigners!'. They wanted to attack them. Lot went out and said, 'Don't attack these people; they are my guests.' They replied, 'You aren't from round here either, and we're going to teach you a lesson.' They were going to break the door down when the messengers blinded all of them. Not one of them could find the doorway any more. Then the two men warned Lot, 'This city has to be destroyed, but God is concerned about you. Escape towards the mountains with your family. And don't look behind you.' So Lot escaped to Soar.

As the sun was rising sulphur and fire fell upon Sodom like a curse from heaven. The ground caved in. The town and its surroundings shook. Then, in a huge earthquake, everything collapsed. There was nothing left, no buildings, plants or people.

Lot's wife looked back to what was behind her. She was rooted to the spot, turned solid, like those strange pillars of salt you find along the shores of the Dead Sea.

Early that morning Abraham went to the place where he had prayed to God. He looked towards Sodom. Smoke was rising from the ground. God had remembered Abraham and had saved Lot. But the punishment had still been very severe.

Isaac and Ishmael

Abraham and Sara were going to have a baby. That was what God promised. But what was going to happen to Ishmael, the child of Abraham and Hagar?

Everything happened just as God had promised. Sara had a new lease of life in her old age, and had a baby boy. She was full of joy, 'Who would have thought it?' she said, 'God has given me something to laugh and smile about.'

Abraham called the child Isaac, which means 'God's smile'. Isaac grew up and on the day he was weaned Abraham had a great party with music and dancing. The singers started to dance; they clapped their hands to give the rhythm and flutes, cymbals and tambourines were played.

Everybody said, 'God remembers the promise, made to Abraham and his descendants for ever.'

Ishmael and his mother Hagar came back to live in Abraham's tribe. Sara saw Ishmael laughing with her son Isaac and she said to Abraham, 'That slave's child should not share your inheritance with my son Isaac. Send them away; get rid of this servant and her son.'

Hagar and Ishmael walked for days and days through the dust under the blazing sun. When they ran out of water, Hagar made her son lie down under a prickly bush, then she went to sit a stone's throw away so as not to have to watch him die. Because that is what happens in the desert when you run out of water. She cried, and howled in despair.

This made Abraham very sad, because Ishmael was also his son. He was torn between his two sons and prayed to God, and God said to him, 'Pay attention to what Sara says to you, because it will be Isaac's descendants who carry your name. But Ishmael is your son too and I will make another nation from his descendants.'

Early in the morning, Abraham gave Hagar bread and water and drove her and Ishmael away. They took the desert road towards Beersheba.

And God heard Ishmael's cries, and called out: 'Hagar, what's the matter? Get up and get the boy up. I shall make a great nation from him.'

God opened Hagar's eyes and she saw a water hole. She got something for her son to drink and quenched his thirst. Ishmael grew up in the desert. He lived in the desert and God was with him.

———

People say it was Ishmael who was the ancestor of the peoples of the Arabian desert, who know the secret paths and can find their way by the stars.

The sacrifice

This is a very well-known story.
The Jewish, Christian and Muslim
traditions teach that it was a terrible test
of Abraham, the father of all believers,
who wanted always to obey God.
Many ancient people used
to kill children as an offering
to their gods. This story
shows that the God of Abraham
refused this offering.

early and saddled his donkey. He cut some logs,
prepared bundles of wood and set off with two
servants and his son Isaac for the place God had
told him.

On the third day, Abraham saw the mountain.
He told his servants to stay with the donkey and
wait, and he said, 'My son and I will go up to
worship God.' Abraham made Isaac carry the
wood for the sacrifice, and he took the embers and
the knife. Off they both went. Isaac called out,
'Father.' And Abraham said, 'Here I am.' Isaac
said, 'I can see the fire and the wood, but where is
the lamb for the sacrifice?' Abraham told his son,
'God will see to that. God sees. God will provide.'

One evening the Lord God put Abraham to the
test. Hearing God's call, Abraham replied, 'Here
I am.' God said, 'Take your son, your dearly loved
son, Isaac. Go to the area of Moriah, and sacrifice
him on the top of the mountain.' Abraham got up

When they arrived on top of the mountain Abraham built an altar for the sacrifice.

Then he tied up his son Isaac.
He put him on the altar.
He took the knife.
He held out his hand to kill his son.
Then he heard God calling him,
'Abraham! Abraham!'
Abraham replied, 'Here I am.'
God said, 'Do not touch your son. Do not harm him. Now I know that you honour me. I have seen your faith. You would have given me your best-loved son.'

Lifting his eyes, Abraham saw a ram tangled in a bush. He caught it and offered it to God as a sacrifice, in place of his son Isaac.

———

Before he left with his son, and before joining his servants and returning to Beersheba, Abraham, they say, gave this place the name: 'God gives what we need.'

What does God give: everything we need like a father or mother.

The succession

Isaac succeeded Abraham
as tribal chief.
He also inherited
the covenant with God.

When Abraham was already very old he called his most faithful servant and said, 'My son is old enough to marry. I don't want him to marry a girl from this area, a Canaanite. Go back to my country and to my own people and choose a wife for my son Isaac.'

The servant replied, 'A woman from down there would not want to come here with me. It would be better if your son came with me.' But Abraham said, 'No, the Lord has promised to give this country to my descendants. My son will stay here. You go alone to my old country and God will help you.'

The servant took in his luggage all the best presents his master could offer. He saddled his camels and set off.

One evening he was resting at the well of Nahor, just at the time when the women came out to get water. He prayed to God, 'Lord, show your friendship for my master Abraham. The young women are coming to the well. When I say to one of them, "Let your water jar down into the well so that I can drink," and she offers to get water for my camels as well, that will be the one you have chosen for Isaac.'

The man had hardly finished his prayer when he saw a very beautiful young woman. He went up to her and said, 'Please could you get me a mouthful of water?' She let down her water jar, 'Please drink,' she said, 'and I'll get water for your camels too until they've had all they want.' The servant was watching out for this, to see if it was a true sign from God. He got some of the jewels out of his luggage, gave them to the young woman and said, 'Who are you? Who is your father? Could you offer a passing traveller somewhere to stay?'

She replied, 'I am Rebecca, daughter of Bethuel and granddaughter of Nahor, the brother of Abraham. You can stay with us.'

Rebecca told her brother Laban about this meeting and he invited the man to stay. He gave him hay for his animals, water to wash his feet, and a meal. The man explained what he was doing. 'I work for Abraham,' he said. 'He is now rich and important. His wife Sara, very late in life gave him an heir, Isaac. And my master has sent me here to find a wife for Isaac. And I believe that Rebecca could be his wife, because God gave me a sign when I met her.'

Laban and Bethuel (Rebecca's father) exclaimed, 'It's the will of God. Let Rebecca marry Isaac.' The servant gave presents to the whole family, and then they ate and drank together. But the next day, when the servant wanted to leave with Rebecca, the family tried to get him to stay a little longer, 'Stay a bit longer,' they said. In the end they asked Rebecca what she thought, 'Do you want to leave with this man?' 'Yes,' she said.

So they said goodbye to Rebecca, and blessed her, saying, 'Grow into a great people, and may you have millions of descendants who can conquer all their enemies.' Rebecca got on to her camel, and, with her old nurse to keep her company, she set off with Abraham's servant.

At that time Isaac had settled near the Negeb. One evening when he was out walking alone in the countryside he saw some camels arriving. It was Rebecca's caravan. When Rebecca saw Isaac she asked, 'Who is that man coming to meet us?'

The servant replied, 'My master, Isaac.' Isaac invited Rebecca into his tent, and she married him. Isaac loved her very much.

By that time Abraham was a hundred and seventy five years old, or so they say. He had had a long and full life, among his people, blessed by God.

Isaac was his dearly-beloved son, the 'son of the promise of God'. Abraham gave Isaac all he had, and then he died happy. His sons Isaac and Ishmael (who had come back from the desert) carried his body into the cave at Machpelah in Hebron, in the tomb of Sara on the land he had bought.

———

This is the end of the stories of Abraham, the father of believers, in which it was proved once and for ever that God is faithful to his promise.

Jacob and Esau

The Bible tells how God
renewed the promise
and told Isaac's wife
Rebecca, 'You will have
two sons, who will be
the ancestors of two
peoples; and the elder
one will serve the younger.'

One day Isaac called Esau and said, 'Go out and hunt for game, and I will bless you before I die.' Off went Esau; but Rebecca had heard this. She said to Jacob, 'Kill two good kids and I will cook them the way your father likes. You can take them to him and he will give you the blessing instead.' Rebecca thought out how to deceive Isaac. She gave Jacob Esau's clothes to put on and covered his arms with goatskin to make them hairy. In disguise, Jacob took the food to his father, and said, 'I am Esau. Eat this game and bless me.' Isaac felt Jacob and was puzzled, 'You have Jacob's voice,' he said, 'but you have Esau's hairy arms.'

Isaac recognized the smell of Esau's clothes, so be blessed Jacob. When Esau came back with the game, he took it to his father. Isaac was horrified, 'Who are you?' he asked. Esau replied, 'Your elder son, Esau.' Isaac trembled, 'I've already given my blessing to the son who brought me the dish.' Esau cried, 'Father, bless me too. It's lucky for Jacob that his name means "God protects".'

That day Esau cried, and vowed to kill his brother Jacob.

Rebecca found out that Esau was vowing to take revenge, and warned Jacob, 'Run away quickly. Go and take refuge with my brother Laban, in Haran.'

The elder son Esau, red-headed and hairy, always used to be out around the countryside. The second son, Jacob, usually stayed peacefully in the camp. One day Esau came home exhausted and hungry, and Jacob was preparing a lentil stew. Esau couldn't resist it, and when Jacob would not give him any he offered Jacob all his rights as elder brother, his inheritance of the promise of God, in return for this stew.

Time passed. Isaac grew old and blind.

So Jacob set off along the road to Haran, the town which Abraham had originally set out from.

One evening it got dark before he had time to reach a village, so he slept in the open air. He had a strange dream in which he saw a ladder going from heaven to earth and messengers from God going up and down it. The Lord God was standing near him and said, 'I am the Lord, the God of Abraham and Isaac. I will give you this land where you are lying. Your descendants will be as many as the grains of sand. And in you all the families of the earth will be blessed. I shall keep my promise.' Jacob woke up terrified, 'God is here,' he thought, 'and I didn't realize.' He took the stone which he had used as a pillow, and set it on end like a milestone, and he called that place Bethel, which means 'house of God'. Then he promised, 'If the Lord is with me, the Lord shall be my God.'

When he arrived in the area of Haran, Jacob saw a well covered with a rock. Three shepherds were waiting until their flocks had all arrived before lifting the rock, and Jacob asked them, 'Where are you from?' They replied, 'From Haran.' Jacob asked for news of Laban, and they pointed out to him Laban's daughter Rachel, who was arriving with her sheep. Jacob rolled the rock off the well so that Rachel's sheep could drink. Then he told her that he was her cousin and gave her a kiss; it was a moment he would never forget. This was how Jacob went to stay with his uncle Laban.

A large family

Even though Jacob had tricked Esau, and had to escape from the land God had promised, he had realized in his dream that God was renewing the promise of a land and a family. Was he still worthy of God's trust?

Jacob then became a shepherd on Laban's farm. A month later, Laban asked him what he wanted to be paid for his work. Now Laban had two daughters: Leah, the elder had a gentle and loving look, but Rachel, the younger one, was beautiful. Jacob was in love with her, and so he told Laban that he would like to work for him for seven years if he could marry Rachel at the end. Seven years seemed like seven days to Jacob because he was so happy to be near his bride.

At the end of the seven years Laban organized a great wedding. According to custom the bride was veiled until the evening; so Jacob could not see her face. But in the evening there was a surprise for him: his wife was . . . Leah.

This time it was Jacob who had been tricked. He complained to Laban, 'What have you done to me? You promised me Rachel as a reward for my work. Why have you tricked me?'

Laban replied, 'In our country it's the custom that the younger sister cannot get married before her elder sister. But if you promise to work for me for seven more years, you can marry Rachel as well.' In that country men could have several wives.

So Jacob agreed to work for Laban for seven more years.

Jacob loved Rachel much more than Leah. God saw Leah's sadness, because she was not loved as much as Rachel.

When Leah got pregnant she thanked God, who had seen her sorrow and had given her children to make Jacob love her more. She had four sons one after the other: Reuben, Simeon, Levi and Judah.

But Rachel could not have children. She became jealous and was so unhappy she wanted to die. According to the custom she asked Jacob if her maid could have a child in her place: in this way Dan and Naphtali were born, and Rachel adopted them as gifts from God. Leah also offered her maid to Jacob as a wife, and her children were Gad and Asher. Then Leah had two more sons, Issachar and Zebulun and one daughter, Dinah.

After all this time Rachel became pregnant and had a son, Joseph. Jacob was the father of a large family, and everything went well for him, and his cousins envied him.

One day Jacob called Rachel and Leah and said, 'Your father is taking advantage of me. God promised that I would go back to my father's country. So let's go.' Jacob waited until Laban was away organizing the sheep shearing, and then escaped with all his family. Laban heard about it three days later and set off to chase Jacob. He caught up with him on the seventh day and said, 'Why did you run away without telling me? We could have had a farewell party. I haven't even had the chance to kiss my daughters and my grandchildren goodbye. You have behaved very stupidly.' Jacob replied, 'I was afraid that you would not want to part from your daughters; in the time I have been working for you, you have not always kept your promises.'

Jacob was upset, and Laban calmed him down: 'I could take revenge, but I know that your God is guiding you. So let's forgive each other.'

Then Jacob and Laban set up a sacred stone and prayed to God to witness their peace treaty.

And Jacob continued his journey towards the land of Canaan, his father's country.

31

The reconciliation

As he returned to his country,
Jacob was afraid that Esau might kill him,
or that he might kill Esau;
he was afraid that he had ruined his life
by his pride;
he was frightened of God,
whom he would not trust.
Making peace with someone
only happens after a struggle.

Jacob sent his family across the Jabbok river and stayed behind on his own. That night someone came to fight with Jacob. During the fight he wounded his thigh. When dawn came, the mysterious stranger said, 'Let me go.' Jacob replied, 'Bless me first'. The stranger asked, 'What is your name?' Jacob said, 'Jacob.' The stranger said, 'From now on you shall be called "Israel", because you have fought with God and won.'

Jacob also asked the stranger's name, but the stranger blessed him without answering.

Jacob called this place 'Penuel' – 'face of God' – because he had seen God face to face and was still alive.

Esau had sworn to get his revenge. A messenger warned Jacob, 'Your brother is coming to meet you with four hundred men.' Jacob was terrified. He divided his tribe into two camps: if Esau attacked one, the other would be able to escape. Then he prayed, 'God of Abraham and Isaac, save us. Esau is going to massacre us.' He sent Esau five hundred and fifty animals one by one as a present, to impress him, please him and calm him down.

The sun was rising when Jacob left Penuel. Like a new-born child he had a new name: 'Israel', which means 'strong before God'.

In the morning Jacob saw Esau arriving with four hundred men. He made his wives and children go behind him. Then he bowed seven times to the ground, and went forward alone towards his brother.

But Esau ran to meet him, threw his arms around him and kissed him. The two brothers wept with joy.

Then Esau saw Leah and Rachel and the children, and asked who they were. Jacob replied, 'These are the children God has given me.' He introduced all of them to his brother, and they all bowed down before Esau.

When he saw this large family, Esau, who was rich and had everything he wanted, didn't want to accept Jacob's presents. But Jacob insisted, 'I beg you, since we have met face to face, just as I met God face to face, and since you have welcomed me with open arms, accept my presents as if they came from God.'

So Esau offered to accompany Jacob, but Jacob refused, saying that the children would walk too slowly. Now they were reconciled the two brothers could part in peace. They would keep in touch with each other. Each of them would go his own way. Esau returned towards Seir, and Jacob set off for Sichem. He and his family walked in the presence of God.

Jacob stopped for the first night, and built huts with branches to shelter his animals. That is why the place is called Succoth, which means 'the huts'. Then he went on to Bethel, where he had dreamed about the ladder. He set up an altar to God who had never abandoned him, and God confirmed the promise, 'Jacob, from now on you will be called "Israel".

'The land which I gave to Abraham and Isaac will be yours, and you will have a multitude of descendants.'

They had set out again when Rachel, who was pregnant, realized that her baby was about to be born. She had a difficult time, and the midwife who was helping her had just the time to tell her, 'You have another son' before she died, there, on the road to Bethlehem. Jacob-Israel buried Rachel, the wife he loved most dearly. He called the baby 'Benjamin'. Now he had twelve sons.

Joseph the innocent victim

**In those days
people believed
that misfortunes
were punishments from God.
So this story is surprising
because God is on the side
of the victim.**

Joseph was seventeen. His father Jacob remembered his son's dreams and wondered if he ought to see in them some signs from God. His brothers, on the other hand, were jealous of him and could not be polite to him. One day Joseph stayed alone with his father while his brothers went off to take the flocks to graze.

Some time after they had gone, Jacob sent Joseph to see if his brothers and their flocks were all right.

So Joseph left Hebron where he lived, to go to Sichem to join his brothers.

When his brothers saw him arriving all alone, they said to each other, 'Here comes the dreamer. We could kill him and say he had been eaten by a leopard.'

Reuben didn't agree: 'No,' he said, 'don't shed blood. Let's throw him down the well.'

When Joseph arrived, they took off the coat of many colours which Jacob had given him. A camel caravan of merchants arrived and Judah said, 'Joseph is our brother after all. Rather than leave him to die, let's sell him to these merchants.'

From then on Jacob lived in Canaan with his twelve sons. One day his favourite son, Joseph, said he had had a strange dream. 'We were in the fields,' he said, 'tying up our sheaves of corn. My sheaf stood straight up, and your sheaves all bowed down in front of it.' His brothers didn't need to ask what this dream meant. They answered, 'Who do you think you are? A king or a master, that we should bow down to you?'

But Joseph told them about another dream; he said, 'The sun, the moon and eleven stars all bowed down in front of me.' This time his father told him off, 'Do you really think we are all going to bow down in front of you?'

Joseph was taken off to Egypt by the merchants to be sold as a slave.

His brothers dipped his tunic in the blood of a bull and took it back to Jacob, who cried and would not be consoled. He only wanted to die, to be reunited with his favourite son.

Meanwhile in Egypt, Joseph was bought by Potiphar, an army officer. When he saw what an efficient servant Joseph was, Potiphar thought, 'God is with him', and he put him in charge of his whole household.

Joseph was very good-looking, and Potiphar's wife fell in love with him. Joseph did not want to deceive his master, but one day, Potiphar's wife grabbed hold of him to kiss him. Joseph pulled away, leaving his coat in her hands. She told her husband, 'Joseph tried to put his arms around me, but I called for help and he ran away.'

Potiphar did not doubt this story. He threw Joseph into prison.

governor trusted Joseph and put him in charge of the prison and gave him a free hand.

It happened just then that Pharaoh's butler and his baker were put in prison. One night, both of them had dreams. The butler said, 'I dreamed that there was a vine with three branches, and there were grapes on it. I crushed the grapes in Pharaoh's cup and gave it to him.' Joseph said, 'That means that in three days you will go back to being Pharaoh's butler. But when you get there, my friend, tell him about me and get him to let me out of prison.' The baker said, 'In my dream I was carrying three baskets of cakes, but the birds ate them.' Joseph told him, 'That means that in three days' time Pharaoh will hang you, and you will be eaten by the birds.'

Three days later, on his birthday, Pharaoh hanged the baker and gave the butler his job back. But the butler forgot Joseph.

Even in prison, God made everything Joseph did a success. Joseph was favourably noticed by the prison governor, and they became friends. The

Joseph, Prime Minister in Egypt

**In those days
people believed
that God spoke to them in their dreams.
Joseph understood the meaning of dreams.
So he seemed
to know the secrets of God.
What would he do with this power?**

of corn are seven years of good harvest and richness. The seven thin cows and the seven thin ears of corn are seven years of famine. God is showing you what is going to happen.'

Two years passed.
One morning Pharaoh asked his priests the meaning of a worrying dream he had had.
But no-one could interpret the dream.
The head butler told him about Joseph, the young foreigner who could interpret dreams. Pharaoh sent for him and told him the dream, 'Seven fat cows were grazing on the banks of the Nile. But seven other cows, thin ones, came along and ate up the fat cows. Then I saw seven beautiful fat ears of corn. But seven others, all thin and dried up, came and swallowed them.' Joseph said, 'Your two dreams are really one dream. The seven fat cows and the seven fat ears

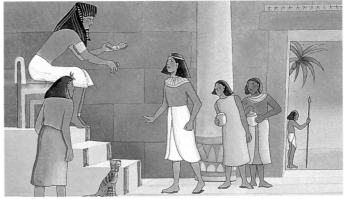

Then Joseph advised Pharaoh to build store-houses during the seven good years and to choose a reliable person to lead the country. Pharaoh said to Joseph, 'Since God has told you all this, there is no one else as wise as you. So I am appointing you Prime Minister; here is my seal and my golden collar.'
During the seven rich years the fields produced good harvests. Joseph built huge store-houses, and stored huge quantities of grain.
Then came the famine. Joseph opened his store-houses and sold the stocks from the earlier years.

When Joseph was thirty he married an Egyptian woman, Asenath. They had two children: Manasseh and Ephraim.

The famine affected neighbouring countries as well, but the news spread, 'There is corn in Egypt.' People came from everywhere to buy corn; from everywhere, even from Joseph's country.

Jacob sent his sons, all except little Benjamin, to Egypt. When they arrived they bowed down before the Prime Minister, Joseph, without recognizing him. But he recognized them, and decided to accuse them of being foreign spies. They explained that they belonged to a family of twelve brothers; one had disappeared, and the youngest had stayed at home. Joseph commanded them, 'Go back to your country and bring me your youngest brother; I will keep Simeon as a hostage.' It was their turn to be in despair. Joseph sent them back with some corn, but he had hidden the money they had paid in their sacks.

When they got home, they told their father about their adventure. When they emptied their sacks they found the money and they were terrified. They remembered how they had once, long ago, sold Joseph as a slave. Now they were being bought and sold.

When Jacob realized that Simeon was missing and that the Egyptian was asking for Benjamin, he cried, 'First I lose Joseph, and now Simeon and Benjamin. Do you want me to lose all my children?' But the famine got worse and there was nothing else they could do but go back to Egypt.

Judah promised that he would bring Benjamin back safely. Jacob let him go, and stayed on his own, like a childless man.

The young people prepared special gifts from their country to give the Egyptian.

They took the money which had been in their sacks after their first visit, and some more money. Then they set off with Benjamin.

Joseph, a saviour

**The end of the Joseph story;
Jacob's family settle in Egypt.
Later their descendants
will tell this story
about how God
saved his people.**

At sunrise the brothers set off for home. But they had not gone far when some Egyptian soldiers, on Joseph's orders, caught them and accused them of stealing, asking them why they did harm in return for kindness.

The brothers denied everything, and even said that if any of them had Joseph's cup in his sack he deserved to die. The soldiers found the cup in Benjamin's sack.

The young men could not understand the disaster that had struck them. They went back shaking with fear.

Benjamin knelt down in front of Joseph. Judah begged, 'Spare us. You see us before you, in disgrace, our hands and feet tied. Make us your slaves.'

But Joseph said he would keep the thief, Benjamin.

Judah who had promised his father that he would not return without his little brother, said, 'Our old father has already lost one son. If you deprive him of his last child, you will kill him. Take me as a slave in his place.'

Joseph's brothers arrived in Egypt for the second time. They were sure that they would be made slaves, and handed over the money from their first trip. To their amazement Joseph set Simeon free and invited them to lunch. Benjamin was treated like a king. Joseph drank from a golden cup and asked for news of their father. He was overwhelmed at seeing Benjamin again, and had to turn away from them to hide his feelings.

He gave orders that their sacks should be filled with corn and that they should be given their money back. Then he hid his own cup in Benjamin's sack.

Then Joseph revealed who he was, 'I am Joseph, your brother. Is our father really still alive?' This took his brothers' breath away.

Joseph repeated, 'I am the brother you sold. Do not feel guilty. It was God sending me here to save lives. Go back quickly and tell our father the news, and bring him here with the whole tribe.'

The brothers went back then to Canaan, but Jacob did not believe them. His heart turned cold with the shock. Then they told him all over again everything that Joseph had said to them. And Jacob saw the chariots, and the food and the animals which Joseph had sent. He began to breathe again. He said, 'Is my son Joseph really still alive? Then I must go. I want to see him before I die.'

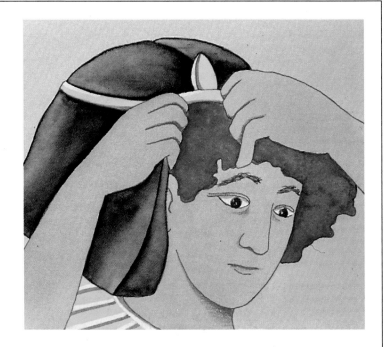

And Jacob-Israel went to Egypt with all his descendants, seventy people altogether. On the way they stopped at Beersheba, and Jacob dreamed that God was calling him: 'I am the God of your father. Do not be afraid to go to Egypt. I shall be there with you and I shall make of you a great people.'

When Joseph heard they were arriving he ran out to meet his father and threw his arms round him. His father said, 'Joseph, I've seen your face again; now I am ready to die, since you are alive.'

Jacob lived there for seventeen years. When he felt death was near he made Joseph promise to take his body to the cave in the field of Machpelah, the tomb of Sara and Abraham, of Isaac and Rebecca, in the Promised Land. Then he blessed Ephraim and Manasseh, Joseph's two sons, 'I thought I would never see you again and

now God has allowed me also to see your children. I am dying. But God will be with you and will bring you back to the land of our fathers.'

At the end Jacob blessed his twelve sons, the chiefs of the twelve tribes of Israel.

Then he lay down and died.

As for Joseph, he was reconciled with his brothers and lived in Egypt long enough to see his great-grandchildren born there.

Rescued and chosen

In the Bible, Moses is the hero of the Book of Exodus, which means 'Way Out'. But the Exodus was a Way Out which led into a whole new history, the history of the people of Israel.

In Egypt the children of Jacob-Israel had children and grandchildren. One day a new Pharaoh came to the throne and said, 'The tribes of Israel are getting too large; they could turn against us, and we could have enemies right inside our own country. We must make them disappear.'

And so Pharaoh forced the people of Israel to build new towns.

Brutal overseers and slave-drivers treated the people like animals.

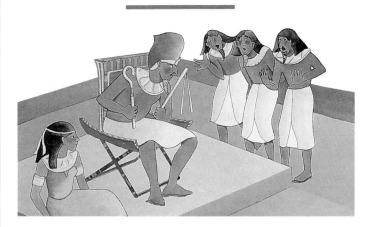

The men had to mould the bricks, bake them, carry them and build with them without stopping. But in spite of their cruel life, the families of Israel continued to grow.

So then Pharaoh told the Egyptian midwives to make sure that all new-born boys died. They did not obey him. So Pharaoh forced all the Egyptians to drown the little Israelite boys in the Nile. Their cries could be heard throughout the country.

One woman hid her baby. And after three months, when hiding him became too difficult, she put him in a basket and hid him in the reeds on the edge of the Nile. The baby's sister hid nearby to see what would happen.

As it happened that day Pharaoh's daughter came down to the river and found the basket floating among the rushes. She realized that this was an Israelite child but decided to save it. Then the sister of the baby came out of hiding and offered to find a nurse for the baby, and ran off to get her mother. In this way the baby was given to its own mother, who had been taken on as a nurse by Pharaoh's daughter. Then the child lived in the palace, and Pharaoh's daughter loved him like her own son. She chose his name, 'Moses', which means 'saved from the waters'.

The people of the tribes of Israel had become Pharaoh's slaves. On the building sites the Egyptian overseers whipped them like animals to make them work.

When Moses grew up, he saw that this forced labour was wrong. One day an Egyptian beat a slave in front of him and he was so horrified he killed the Egyptian.

Moses had to run away, and he took refuge in the country of the Midianites. There he married the daughter of Jethro, a priest who had welcomed him.

One day Moses was taking the sheep to graze on Mount Horeb. A bush burst into flame but was not burnt. Moses went near and heard a voice, 'Moses, I am the God of your fathers and mothers.' Moses was afraid to look into God's face. God said, 'I have seen the misery of my people. I want to set them free. Go: I am sending you to lead them out of Egypt.' Moses interrupted, 'Why me?' God went on, 'I am with you.' Moses hesitated, 'If I say to the chiefs of the tribes of Israel, "The God of your mothers and fathers has sent me to you", they are going to ask me your name.' God said, 'I am who I shall be. You will say "I am" sent you. It is my name.' Moses argued further that he was not good at making speeches. God grew angry, 'I will give you the words you need,' God said, 'and your brother Aaron will help you. He certainly knows how to make speeches.'

So Moses accepted this mission.

The people of Israel quickly came to trust him, but Pharaoh was not impressed. When Moses and Aaron said to him, 'The God of Israel asks you to let our people go to celebrate a feast in the desert', he replied, 'Who is this God? Why should I do what this God says?' He refused, and made them work even more.

The people of Israel were oppressed even more than before, and they blamed Moses, 'It's your fault,' they said, 'Pharaoh is going to work us to death.'

So Moses turned to God: 'Lord, why did you send me?' he asked. 'All I've done is make the oppression of my people worse.'

The Lord replied, 'I will lead you out of Egypt. You shall be my people and I will be your God.'

God passes over

Pharaoh had refused
to let the tribes of Israel
leave Egypt.
Strange events then happened,
which the Bible calls
'signs of God'.
This is the epic of the ten plagues
of Egypt, like a long war
between two stubborn enemies
Pharaoh and God.

Moses' brother Aaron threw his stick in front of Pharaoh and it turned into a snake. But the Egyptian magicians did the same thing, and Pharaoh Hard-Heart did not give in.

Aaron struck the river Nile with his stick and all the waters turned into blood. The fish died. The Egyptians had nothing to drink; all their water jars were full of blood. But the Egyptian magicians did the same thing and Pharaoh's heart grew harder. The whole of Egypt was overrun by frogs; they swarmed and got into everything; they climbed on everything. Pharaoh promised that if the frogs disappeared he would let the people of Israel go. The frogs died. But Pharaoh Hard-Heart did not keep his promise.

Then the whole of Egypt was plagued by mosquitoes, flies, fleas. Pharaoh gave way, but as soon as the plague was gone, he became stubborn again.

The flocks of the tribes of Israel flourished, while the Egyptians' animals fell sick with the plague: horses, donkeys, bulls, sheep, all died.
Pharaoh Hard-Heart did not give in.

The Egyptians fell sick. They got boils from the polluted air. They were covered with oozing sores. Pharaoh Hard-Heart did not give way.

The Lord sent hail over Egypt; no one had ever seen such hailstones. Hailstones fell on people, animals and vegetables, on the barley and the flax. Pharaoh saw he was wrong. He seemed to be ready to let the tribes of Israel go. But as soon as the hail stopped, Pharaoh Hard-Heart refused.

The Lord sent a swarm of locusts over Egypt. They ate everything that was still there after the hail storm. Not a green leaf was left. Pharaoh asked Moses to pray to God to get rid of the locusts. But as soon as the last locust was gone Pharaoh became stubborn again.

Then for three days it was dark in Egypt. The country was covered in darkness as if God had never created light and separated it from darkness. Egypt was like the country of the blind.

Pharaoh Hard-Heart, more stubborn than ever, would not yield. He refused to let the people go.

God said to Moses, 'I am going to send one last plague on Egypt, and Pharaoh will send you away. Each family should kill a lamb and make a mark on the door with its blood. Roast it with bitter herbs and eat it; make bread without leaven. Put on your travel clothes before you do all this. I am going to pass over the country. This will be the Passover of God.' The people of Israel followed God's commands. And that night God passed over all the houses marked by the blood of the lamb. But in all the other houses a great cry tore the night apart. The Egyptians were howling in despair: in every family the eldest son was dying.

In Pharaoh's palace the eldest son, the heir to the throne, died like the rest. Pharaoh's hard heart was broken. In the middle of the night his heart became gentle and he sent for Moses and Aaron. He gave the long-awaited order, 'Tribes of Israel, get up and go away from my people, go and serve your God.' And the tribes of Israel went, without even waiting for their bread to rise.

It was the fourteenth day of the first month, in spring.

Passing over to freedom

This was the most important event
in history. As in the first
Creation story God separated
the sea from the land.
Passing through the sea was
a new creation, the creation of a
people whom God had brought
through death to life.
This was the real beginning of
the history of the people of Israel.

The people of Israel left Egypt in a long caravan, which trailed along behind Moses towards the Red Sea. He went forward, sure that God was there, near them and yet hidden: in daytime a pillar of cloud led the way; at night a pillar of fire lit their path.

When Pharaoh heard they had gone his heart became more stony than ever. He ordered six hundred of his fastest chariots to be prepared and set off in pursuit. While the people were encamped beside the sea, some men saw the Egyptian army galloping towards them. Trapped between the enemy and the sea they cried to Moses, 'Did you know what you were doing when you brought us out of Egypt? We're all going to die here.' Moses reassured them, 'Do not be afraid. God will save us.' Already the pillar of cloud was moving between the Egyptians and the Israelite camp. Then Moses stretched out his hand over the sea, and all night long the Lord God made the sea roll back; a violent east wind made the seabed dry.

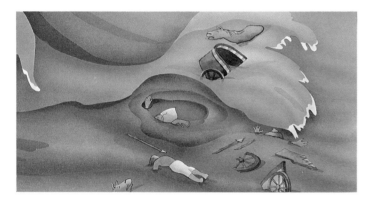

The waters parted. There was a passage leading between the waves, like a road in the middle of the sea. The people of Israel crossed the sea without getting their feet wet, and the waters formed a wall to the right and to the left. The Egyptians rushed after them, and all Pharaoh's horses and men and chariots advanced into the sea.

Their wheels began to sink into the soft seabed, and they came to a halt, stuck in the wet sand. As soon as Moses was sure that God was saving them, he stretched out his hand again over the sea, and the water flowed back in huge waves into its normal place. Although the tribes of Israel had crossed the sea with dry feet, the waves now overwhelmed the chariots and the horsemen. Pharaoh's whole army drowned in the sea. Not one of his soldiers was left.

On that day the people of Israel were sure that they had been saved by God and put their trust in Moses, God's servant.

Some women got out their tambourines and started to dance, and everyone sang, 'God is our strength, and has saved us. Sing to God, who has done marvellous things. The horse and his rider have been thrown into the sea.'

The journey in the desert

Travelling through the desert,
going through joy
and sorrow,
anger and happiness,
doubts and discoveries,
without giving up hope;
that's what faith in God is all about.

The people of Israel went forward into the desert. The sharp stones cut their feet. Their heads were heavy under the hot sun. Their eyes were full of the dust that swirled up in the wind. Their lips were cracked and their mouths were dry. They were overcome with thirst. For three days they had been without water. In the end they arrived at a stream, but the water was bitter and undrinkable. It was the brook of Mara, which means 'bitter'. The people were discouraged and turned against Moses, 'Water!' they shouted. Moses turned to God and God showed him a special tree: Moses threw a few leaves into the water and the bitterness disappeared and the water was drinkable. At last they could drink and be refreshed. This journey across the desert was like an obstacle race. It was as if the Lord God was using this journey through the bare landscape of the desert to strip bare the secrets of everyone's heart; he seemed to want to know if the people loved him enough to trust and obey him. Or was it that the Lord wanted each one, in the emptiness of the desert, to discover what was in her or his own heart?

The people set off again, one by one, avoiding horned vipers, scorpions and green lizards. The heat brought out the sweat on their skins, and sapped their energy.

They were everywhere. You could go on a whole day's journey and still not get away from them. It took two days and a night just to pick them all up. Some people dried them to make them last longer. Everybody ate their fill and more, until they were sick of them.

And the people continued their journey, feet in the dust, hungry again, complaining again. One evening Moses renewed his pledge of trust in God, and said: 'You realize that it is God who brought you out of Egypt. In the morning you shall see the glory of God.'

In the morning the desert of Sin was covered with an amazing dew. When it dried it crackled underfoot like hoar frost. 'What is this?' asked the people and Moses said, 'You've been complaining about being hungry and wishing you were back in Egypt, and murmuring against God. Now look and see the bread God has given you. Pick as much as you want, but don't keep any in reserve; you'll find it each morning, except on the seventh day of the week, the day of rest.' The people of Israel called this bread 'manna' which means 'what's this?' Each morning they picked the manna they needed. It was like white grains and tasted like honey-cake. The people ate it all through their time in the desert, until they arrived in the countryside on the edge of the land of Canaan.

They rebelled against Moses, and said, 'Who will give us meat? When we were in Egypt at least we had fish to eat, cucumbers, and melons and leeks.' Moses was distressed and prayed to God: 'I didn't bring these people into the world. Why do I have to carry them about and feed them, like a mother with her baby? I'd rather die.'

God said to Moses, 'Choose seventy elders. I will give them my Spirit, as I have given it to you, and they will share your burden. As for meat, I'll give them meat until it's coming out of their ears.'

Then he sent a wind from the sea, which grounded a flock of quails. They fell in hundreds.

The Ten Commandments of the Covenant

After the covenant between
God and Noah and the covenant
with Abraham, God made a
covenant with the people
of Israel, and to celebrate this gave
them a present: God's law.

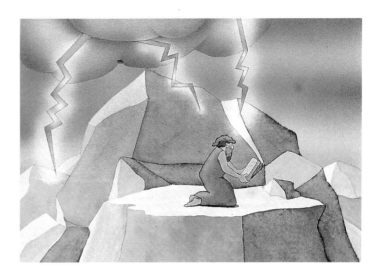

Then, alone, Moses climbed the mountain. There, on the summit, he received the ten commandments of the law for living God's covenant. The words of the covenant were written on stones, the 'Tablets of the Law.'

'I am your God. You shall have no other God. You shall not make idols. You shall respect the name of God and the Day of the Lord. You shall deal rightly with others.' Moses came down the mountain. But he had been up there a long time and the people had given up waiting.

In his absence they had rebelled. They had melted down all their jewellery and had made a golden statue of a calf. They were kneeling down in front of it and dancing in honour of this idol: a god who could be seen and touched.

Three months after they left Egypt, the tribes of Israel reached the Sinai desert. Moses told them, 'God has brought us here, like an eagle carrying us on its wings. God is coming to meet us. Listen to God because we shall be the people of God.'

On the third day a mist settled on the mountain; there were claps of thunder and flashes of lightning, and everyone was afraid.

Moses made the people leave the camp and led them to the foot of the mountain which was covered in mist. God was there.

God spoke with Moses face to face as a friend speaks with a friend. God gave the Ten Commandments all over again, and Moses carved them on the stone tablets. Moses spent forty days with God, and then he went back down the mountain, carrying the two Tablets of the Law. He had met God face to face, and God was shining out of him. He was transformed, glowing, transfigured and altogether changed, a new person. When the others saw him they were full of respect for this hero.

Moses covered his face with a veil, and only took it off when he spoke with God.

Moses saw the calf and the dancing. He saw that the people had already broken the law against making images of God.

He broke the Tablets of the Law, just as the people had broken their covenant with God. Then he attacked the golden calf, broke it to pieces and ground it into dust. He would have liked to choke the people with the evil they had done.

But he did not want to cut the people off from God. He remembered God's promise to Abraham. So when he had severely punished the guilty ones who had started it all, he went back up the mountain to ask God to write his laws on two new tablets of stone.

God had seen that the people were stiff-necked and would not obey, and wanted to destroy them, but Moses begged God to forgive them. He bowed his head to the ground and trusted in God's love for the people. And God forgave them.

To keep the Law of the Covenant with them always, the people of Israel made a box of acacia wood covered in gold, with a gold lid decorated with two angels face to face, watching over the box. From that time on, men carried this box on their shoulders, as a boat is carried by the waves. They called it 'The Ark of the Covenant'. It was the sign that God was mysteriously present in the midst of them. It was the place where God lived among the people.

The last difficulties

The epic drew to an end.
Even so,
people rebelled
and wanted to return to a false paradise
which they thought they had lost.
It's a struggle
to reach the Promised Land.
Is that what it is like getting
into the Kingdom of God?

The desert stretched out to the horizon and every day the horizon seemed further away. The thirst and the exhaustion went on. Again the people complained to Moses: 'Did you make us leave Egypt to die of thirst, and our children too? Get us something to drink. If God is with us, as you say, prove it. Or let God prove it, if God is really with us.' Once again Moses, who relied on God the way

a person leans on a rock, turned to God: 'Lord, what can I do? If this goes on much longer they'll kill me.'

God told Moses to strike the rock with his stick, and from the rock came a spring of water, and the people were able to drink.

Moses called this place 'Massah and Meribah' which mean 'testing and complaint', because the people of Israel put God to the test and complained to Moses.

The next thing that happened was that the desert Bedouins, the Amalekites, attacked. Moses ordered his lieutenant Joshua to take command and he took up his position on the top of the hill with Aaron and Hur.

While Moses held up his arms towards heaven the people of Israel were winning the battle, but when Moses let his arms fall the Amalekites started to get the advantage. But Moses' arms were getting tired: Aaron and Hur had to hold them up until sunset.

That is how the people of Israel beat the Amalekites.

Moses sent spies to explore the land of Canaan, the 'Promised Land'. They came back with a wonderful bunch of grapes and reported, 'It's a land flowing with milk and honey, covered with vines and fig trees. But there are Amalekites living there, and Canaanites and Anakims, real giants. Compared to them we're like grasshoppers.'

All the Israelites' hopes were dashed. They started to weep like abandoned children, and then grew angry: 'God has let us down. Let's turn

After many battles, and many wanderings, and many years, the remnant of the people of Israel finally reached the plains of Moab, facing the Promised Land. There, they couldn't believe their eyes. Their parched mouths shouted for joy, their worn knees found the strength to dance to the glory of God, who was faithful to the promise. Then Moses spoke to Joshua, 'Courage. It's you who will enter the Land which God has promised, with the people.'

Moses entrusted the people to Joshua, and Joshua to God.

And there, on Mount Nebo, Moses died.

There was never another person like Moses in the whole of Israel, and he died before he could enter the Promised Land.

Perhaps the Promised Land was not just this fertile countryside; perhaps Moses' death took him into the promised land of the Kingdom of God.

back,' they said. Although God was slow to anger, he was enraged by this: 'How long will this people refuse to trust me?' he asked. 'I shall take away their inheritance.' Moses reasoned with God: 'These people are your own children,' he said. 'Remember how you love your people.' God said, 'Since you regret crossing the desert, you can spend the rest of your life in it. Only your children will enter the Promised Land with Joshua.'

23

Joshua the conqueror

Joshua is the same name as 'Jesus' which means 'God saves', and the Book of Joshua tells the story of the beginning of the conquest of Canaan, the 'Promised Land', starting 1230 years before the birth of Jesus.

Joshua took over from Moses, and began by sending two spies to find out about the town of Jericho.

The two spies went to visit Rahab, a woman who lived in a house on the city wall. But the King of Jericho heard that the spies had arrived.

He sent soldiers to Rahab's house; but too late. She had already managed to hide the two Israelites on her balcony behind a pile of flax she had harvested. She said that the spies had run away and that the soldiers should chase them. When the soldiers were gone she went to talk to the spies and told them that she knew about their God. 'God brought you out of Egypt,' she said.

'Your God is the only God of Heaven and Earth. I have been straight and honest with you, so will you do the same for me? I saved you from the soldiers; please save my family when you attack Jericho. Swear you will.'

The men swore, 'If you do not betray us, we will protect your family.' Then Rahab helped them to get out of her window and climb right down the city walls, and pointed out a way to get away and hide in the mountains. The two men spent three days in a secret place and then got back safe and sound to the Israelite camp to tell Joshua what they had found out.

Thus they crossed the river on dry ground, to enter the Promised Land, and they celebrated the Passover and ate the unleavened bread and the fruits of the Promised Land. The manna, which God had given them every day, was no longer needed, and stopped appearing. A new world was beginning.

The tribes of Israel had to cross the river Jordan, which was swollen with melted snow.

Joshua announced that God was going to do marvellous things, then he lined up the people for a procession. In front, the priests carried the Ark of the Covenant. As soon as their feet touched the water, the river stopped flowing. While the Ark of the Covenant remained in the river bed the river did not flow.

The gates of Jericho were shut for fear of the Israelites. Their attack on Jericho was like a religious service. They solemnly processed around the city once a day for six days. The procession was in this order: first the outriders, then seven priests carrying rams' horns, then the Ark of the Covenant and the rear guard. On the seventh day they went round seven times. The seventh time they sounded the horns, the people shouted their war cry and, all of a sudden, the walls fell down.

Only Rahab and her family survived, from the whole population of Jericho. And the news travelled: Israel's strength comes from God.

While they were crossing, twelve men, one from each tribe, picked up twelve rocks. When they stopped at Gilgal they set up these rocks in memory of their entry into the Promised Land.

It was the fourteenth day of the first month, the anniversary of the first passover to freedom when the people had crossed the Red Sea without getting their feet wet.

24

Gideon, the warrior

**The Book of Judges
tells how God chose good
people as guides for
the people who settled in
Canaan. One of these
judges was Gideon.**

When the tribes of Israel arrived in the Promised Land they mixed with the local people. Gradually they began to worship the local idols. At Ophrah they bowed down before Baal, who claimed to be the master of the world. So when the Midianites attacked their villages the people of Israel said, 'It is a judgment from God.'

At Ophrah there lived a man called Gideon. One day he heard God speaking to him, 'Gideon, the Lord is with you.' Gideon didn't believe his ears; he said, 'If the Lord is with us, why don't wonderful things happen, as in the past?' God said, 'Go and save Israel from the Midianites.' Gideon replied, 'Lord, my family is the weakest in the tribe, and I am the youngest in the family. If you are really on my side, prove it.' He prepared a tray with some meat and some unleavened bread on it. A flame suddenly burnt up this offering of Gideon's and so he was sure that God was with him.

Secretly, during the night, he destroyed the statue of Baal. Then he sacrificed a bull to God.

The next day the people of Ophrah found their idol Baal in pieces, and their hopes in shreds.

They quickly found out who was to blame and they decided to kill Gideon. But his father protected him and spoke scornfully to his neighbours, 'Don't make me laugh,' he said, 'if Baal is really a god, he doesn't need you to defend him. He can defend himself. Leave Gideon alone.'

conversation: a Midianite was saying, 'I had a dream that a big loaf fell on my tent and squashed it flat.' Another explained, 'This loaf represents the tribe of Gideon, which grows corn. The tent means us, the nomads. Israel is coming, to squash us flat.'

Gideon understood that God would give him the victory. He divided the men into three groups, and gave each group a trumpet, an empty jar and a torch. He told them to shout 'The sword of the Lord and of Gideon!' and sound the trumpets, break the jars and raise the torches; all this was to happen suddenly when they got near the Midianite camp.

And Gideon again asked God to prove that he was on his side. So God gave him another sign. One evening Gideon spread out a sheepskin on the ground: in the morning the ground was completely dry, but there was dew all over the wool. In the evening Gideon again put the sheep's fleece on the ground, and in the morning the ground was all covered with dew and the fleece was bone dry. A sign indeed.

Then, once he was sure that God was his strength, Gideon decided to attack the Midianites. He called on the other tribes of Israel to support him. So many men turned up that Gideon could take his pick of the most self-reliant. Then he went off to spy on the enemy camp. It was like an anthill. Gideon overheard a

That night Gideon's three groups went out and surrounded the Midianite camp. Suddenly they sounded the trumpets, broke the jars, brandished the torches and shouted, 'The sword of the Lord and of Gideon!'

The Midianites were in a terrible panic; they rushed in all directions. The whole camp tried to run away: a real defeat.

Throughout the rest of Gideon's life they were never heard of again; the country was at peace. Those who had followed Gideon asked him to be their king, but Gideon refused, 'God is the only king of Israel,' he said.

25

Samuel, Saul and David

**The tribes of Israel
were determined to have a king
like their neighbours.
Was God not enough
for them?**

Samuel was a judge and a prophet: that means someone who speaks the words of God. He used to visit the tribes of Israel and warn them, 'If you have a king he will make you join the army and pay taxes. The real and only king of Israel is God.' But God said he must listen to the people. And when Saul, a young man from the country, came to visit Samuel, Samuel heard God whisper to him, 'This is the man who will be able to rule my people.' The next day Samuel anointed Saul as king: he poured oil over his head, saying, 'God has chosen you to be the chief among his people. This oil will sink into your skin and show how God's Spirit is entering your life. You are "the Lord's anointed".'

And Samuel presented Saul to the whole people, and said, 'God, who brought us out of Egypt is our king; but God has chosen Saul to be king for you.'

Saul made war on the Moabites, the Ammonites, the Edomites, the Philistines; and then he also attacked the Amalekites. Samuel told him that it was God's will that he should destroy them entirely. With two thousand footsoldiers, Saul attacked; it was a massacre.

Saul destroyed everything . . . or nearly everything. He spared the best animals to sacrifice them to the Lord.

But Samuel said to him, 'It was God who made you king. And he told you to destroy everything. So why have you not done that?'

Saul explained, 'I did what the people wanted. They wanted to please God.'

Samuel replied, 'Do you believe that God likes sacrifices better than obedience? Since you have rejected God's command, God has rejected you, and will find another king.' Saul went back home. The Spirit of God left him, and he went mad.

Samuel was sent by God to Bethlehem, and went to visit Jesse, who had eight sons. Samuel chose to anoint David, the youngest; and from that time on David was the Lord's anointed. God does not care about appearances or strength or height. God sees the heart.

David went to work for Saul, the mad king, to calm him down by playing the lyre. But war broke out again between Philistines and Israelites.

One day the two sides were camping opposite each other. A Philistine soldier called out, 'What is the point of all of us fighting. You choose a hero to fight for you, against me. If he kills me, we will be your slaves. If I kill him, you shall be our slaves.' This was Goliath. He was three metres tall, and wore full armour: greaves, a bronze helmet and a breastplate weighing sixty kilos. The Israelite fighters were terrified. But David said to Saul, 'I'll fight with him.' Saul refused, 'You are only a child.' David insisted, 'I was a shepherd. I've killed lions and bears when they

attacked my flock. Goliath is nothing. The Lord has saved me from the wild beasts, and he will save me from this monster.' David took his sling and chose five stones and walked towards Goliath.

Goliath roared with laughter, 'Come here, little feller,' he shouted, 'I am going to make mincemeat out of you.'

David did not let himself show fear, 'You've only got a lance,' he shouted, 'I've got the strength of God.'

The giant moved forward; David aimed his sling. The stone hit Goliath right in the middle of his forehead. The giant staggered, toppled and fell. David ran up to Goliath, took his sword and cut off his head. When they saw their hero was dead, the Philistines ran away.

It was a triumph for David.

The women came out to meet him, singing: 'Saul has slain his thousands, but David his ten thousands.'

From that day on, Saul was jealous of David: he was afraid that this lad who had only just come up from the country, might become king in his place.

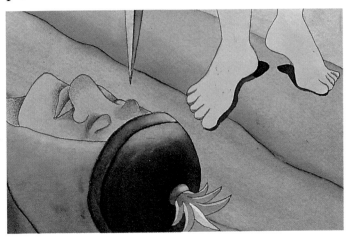

26

David's reign

**David was anointed by Samuel
to show he was God's Chosen One;
he was going to bring the tribes of Israel
together in a single kingdom.
This was about a thousand years
before the birth of Jesus.**

Saul was still pursuing David. But it was David who took Saul by surprise. One night all of Saul's camp were asleep. David and his friend Abishai crept up on the camp. David found Saul asleep, his lance beside him. Abishai wanted to take the opportunity to kill Saul, but David said, 'It is not right to kill the Lord's Chosen One, his anointed.' But he took away Saul's lance and his gourd.

Saul now saw David as a rival who had to be got rid of.

So David had to go and hide in a cave with his family and a group of people who were against the king.

But someone betrayed him and told Saul where he was.

David escaped into the desert of Ziph, and then into the gorge of Engeddi. There were waterfalls there, where antelopes and leopards came to drink. David prayed and sang.
'They have laid a snare for me in my path.
But I cried to you, O Lord. You are my shelter.
As a deer longs for the water brooks,
so longs my soul for you, O Lord.
My soul is athirst for God.'

In the morning David stood on an overhanging rock and called the army chief, 'What a fine guard you have. I could have killed the king. Look, I've taken his lance and his gourd.' Saul was overwhelmed, and he came forward and said, 'David, my son, you could have taken revenge and you didn't. So you care about my life. Forgive my mistakes; I have behaved like a madman. Come back and join me.' David refused. He gave Saul back his lance, and went away, hoping that God cared as much for his own life as he had cared for Saul's.

David set up his capital in Jerusalem, the fortress of the Jebusites, on Mount Zion. He called it 'the city of David'.

He took the Ark of the Covenant there. The Ark entered Jerusalem amid cheers and fanfares. David danced in front of the Ark. He offered sacrifices of peace to the Lord. Then he blessed the people and gave everybody cakes, dates and grapes.

As soon as David had moved into his own house, he realized that he should also build a house for the Ark of God. But a prophet, Nathan, came from God to tell him, 'It is not you who will build me a house; I shall build your house: your descendants will rule for ever. All who descend from your family will be my children, and I will be their father.'

Soon after this a terrible battle took place at Gilboa between the Philistines and Israel. The Israelites fled. The Philistines followed them closely. They killed Jonathan, Saul's son, who was David's best friend, and his two brothers. Saul killed himself. A man ran to tell David about the massacre. David cried all day until the evening, 'Jonathan, how I cared about you. Jonathan, my brother, I loved you so much. Your friendship for me was wonderful.'

Then David went to live at Hebron, near the tomb of Sara and Abraham. The people of the tribe of Judah made him their king. Seven years later, the elders of all the tribes came to fetch him, and said, 'When Saul was our king, all the women of Israel sang about your victory over Goliath and the Philistines. And God spoke about you and said, "He will be the shepherd, and the chief of my people." '

And they proclaimed David king of Israel, king of all the tribes of the south and the north, chosen by God for his whole people.

27

In the time of exile

**Four hundred years had passed
since the time of David.
The kingdom was divided.
In 587 BC
the armies of Nebuchadnezzar,
king of Babylon,
besieged Jerusalem.
Had God abandoned his people?**

fields will be farmed, the ruins will be rebuilt. I shall bring my people back to their land. I shall give you a new heart, and put a new spirit in you.' Another prophet gave them back their confidence, 'People say, "God has forgotten us". Does a mother forget her baby? Even if she forgets, I, God, will not forget.'

There are stories from later on about how other Jews gave an example of faith, such as Daniel, Hananiah, Azariah and Mishael.

The King of Babylon wanted them to work for him, so he had them taught the Babylonian writing so that they could be astrologers and tell him the future. But the Babylonian cooks did not respect the sacred laws about Jewish food, and so these men refused to eat the dishes which were forbidden to Jews. This was their way of being faithful to God's law.

The walls gave way. They put out the eyes of Zedekiah, the king of Jerusalem, slaughtered many of the people, looted the Temple of God and burnt the city. Many of the survivors had to go into exile in Babylon.

Jeremiah, the prophet of doom, convinced them that all this was the result of their disobeying God. They endured it, keeping in their hearts the promises of Jeremiah, prophet of hope, 'God forgives. One day God will make a new covenant with the people.'

Beside the rivers of Babylon they sat down and wept; the tears ran down their faces when they thought of Jerusalem. The priest Ezekiel promised them that God would do wonders, 'The

men. They sang, 'Bless the Lord, praise him and sing his praises for ever.'

King Nebuchadnezzar was amazed. He had them brought out of the furnace. Their hair wasn't even singed. So the King was impressed with the God of the Jews. He swore: 'From now

King Nebuchadnezzar had a huge gold statue made: and he insisted that everyone should bow down and worship this idol. If not, they would be burnt alive. Hananiah, Azariah and Mishael refused to do this, and proclaimed the faith of Israel, 'The Lord our God is the only God.' Nebuchadnezzar was furious. He ordered the furnace to be lit, and had the men thrown into it. The furnace was so hot that the soldiers who

on, anyone who speaks ill of this God shall be cut in pieces, because there is no other god like this God.'

A few years later, King Cyrus allowed the exiled Jews to return to their country and rebuild their Temple. Was it God who inspired this new king of Babylon?

There was an outburst of joy. Beside the rivers of Babylon the families of Israel got up and organized themselves into convoys, like torrents after a storm. It was like a dream. And those who saw them leave said, 'God has done great things for them.'

pushed them in were burnt to death. But not the three. Azariah prayed, 'Lord, remember your covenant; keep us safe; then they will all know that you are the only God in the world.' The soldiers stirred up the fire. Then an angel from God appeared in the furnace with them, and it felt like a morning breeze and cooled down the

28

Judith the brave

**Judith –
her name means 'the Jewess' –
is the heroine of a story
which celebrates the power of faith.**

In the days when the Assyrians wanted to take over the whole world, on the road to Jerusalem, the army of General Holophernes was encamped near Bethulia. They took control of all the water supplies and the people of Bethulia were dying of thirst; first of all the babies died. Holophernes surrounded the town. There was nothing left in the shops. The children were so hungry they could no longer stand. The people were in despair: 'God has given us up,' they said. 'It would be better to go out and fight than to stay in here doing nothing and watching our children die.'

Ozias their mayor said, 'Let us have faith in God. If nothing has happened in five days we'll go and fight.'

Judith, a very beautiful widow, spoke to the leaders: 'Who do you think you are to set deadlines for God? Have faith in God as Abraham did.' The elders admired Judith. She did not keep God's law carefully, but she knew God better than they did. Judith prayed, 'O God of my father, your strength is not in military power. You are the God of the children, the weak and those who have no hope. Help me, because I'm on my own. Protect Israel.'

Then she put on her best dress, her jewels and perfume, and did her hair. She filled a basket with rolls, cakes, and dried fruit, gave her maid a goatskin of wine to carry, and set off.

Her neighbours were amazed when they saw her so beautifully dressed up, and they were happy for her. They followed her with their eyes as she left the town and went towards the enemy camp.

put the head of Holophernes in her food basket, and left with her maid as if she was going out to pray. But they left the camp altogether and went to Bethulia.

Judith arrived at the Assyrian camp. She told Holophernes that she had run away from Bethulia to join the winning side. She offered to show the Assyrians the little paths that led into Jerusalem. Holophernes was under her spell; he found her a tent in his camp and even let her leave the camp on her own at regular intevals to pray to her God.

When Judith opened the basket, the people couldn't believe it. They exclaimed, 'Blessed are you among women. You will be remembered for ever.' At dawn they hung the head of Holophernes on the ramparts. The Assyrians were thrown into chaos: no general, no army; they fell apart completely. The news reached Jerusalem and a great feast was organized in honour of Judith and to the glory of God.

  The people sang,
'I will sing a new song to God.
God has done marvellous things.
God alone is God.
God's word creates the world,
God's breath gives life.'

  When she had been there for four days he held a feast and invited Judith. Holophernes was very excited, and could only think of one thing: to get Judith into his arms. The banquet started. Because of her religion Judith only ate her own food. Holophernes drank a lot more wine than he was used to, and Judith was watching him. In the end he passed out on his bed, completely drunk.
  Then Judith went up to him, took his sword, grabbed him by the hair and cut off his head. She

29

Jonah the missionary

Here is a surprising and funny story, which the Jews told to show that God is the God of the whole world.

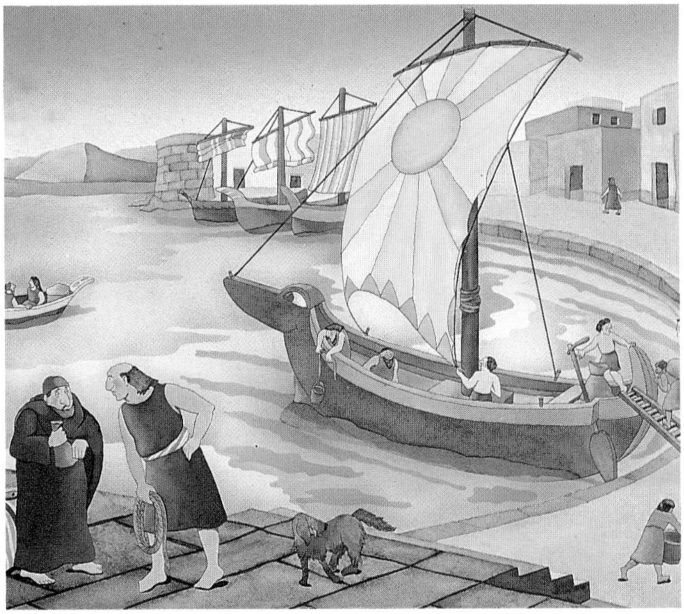

There was once a man named Jonah. He wanted to run away anywhere in the world to escape God's command: God had told him, 'Jonah, get moving. Go to Nineveh and tell the wicked people there that I am angry with them.'

Jonah felt this might be a dangerous thing to do, so he went to Joppa and found a ship going in the opposite direction, to Tarsus.

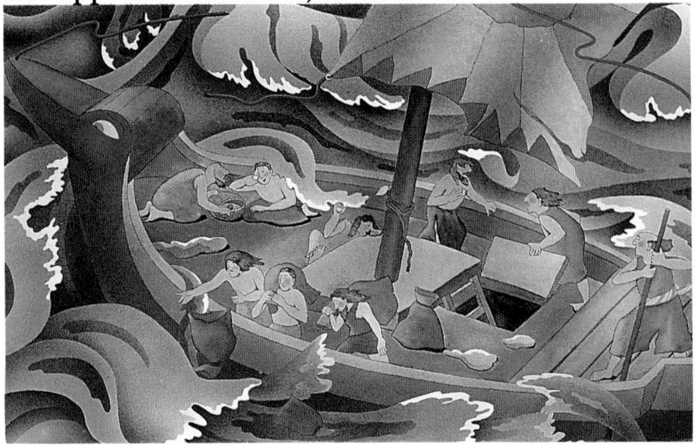

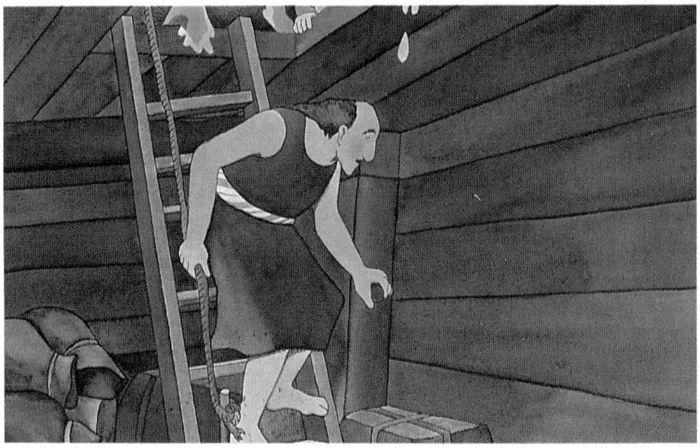

The ship put out to sea, but God let loose a terrible storm. The ship was thrown about by huge waves, and the sailors were afraid. Each one called on his own god for help.

To lighten the ship they threw everything, even the cargo, overboard. But the ship seemed likely to break up and the crew wanted to know who it was who had brought God's anger upon them.

They pulled names out of a hat, and the name was Jonah. The sailors went down to look for him in the bottom of the ship where he was cowering. 'Who are you?' they asked. 'What are you doing here? What have you done to make God send us such a disaster?'

Jonah said, 'My God is the God of the Jews. I am running away from God's command. Everything is my fault. Throw me overboard and you'll be all right.'

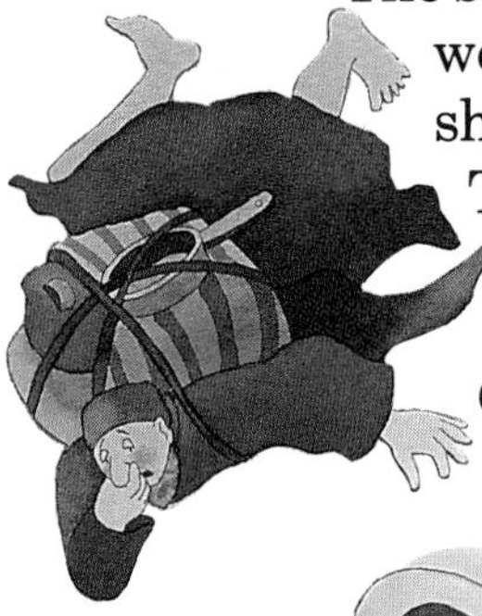

The sailors hesitated, but the waves were coming over the side. The ship seemed to be breaking up. Their only thought was to save their lives. So now they were convinced that it was Jonah's God who had put them into this terrible situation, they pulled Jonah up onto the deck and threw him overboard.

At that very moment a huge fish came along and

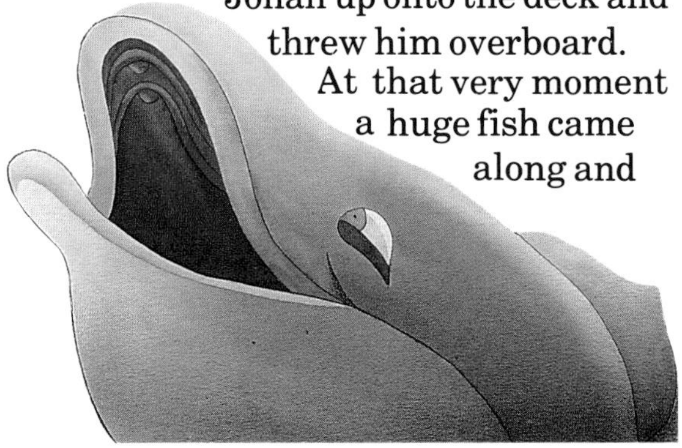

swallowed Jonah. And the sea grew calm.

Jonah spent three days and three nights in the fish's stomach. It was like being buried alive, or in hell.

He prayed, 'Out of the deep I call on you, O God. From the jaws of death I cry and you hear my voice. I am overwhelmed in deep waters, and I have come to a place from which no traveller returns. The waters have covered me and taken my breath from me. But you can bring me out alive.'

Then the fish sicked Jonah up on dry land. And Jonah heard God's command again, 'Get up and go to Nineveh to give them my message.'

Jonah seemed to have risen from the dead. He had become a new man. He went to Nineveh.

When he got to Nineveh he ran along the streets and stopped in the squares, and the people heard him cry, 'In forty days Nineveh will be completely destroyed.' Strangely, they didn't get angry with him . Not only did they listen to him, but they started to believe in God. They were converted. They changed their whole way of life. They made peace among themselves, and those who had treated others unjustly made amends. The important people let the little people go in front of them. It was the world turned upside down. So God decided not to destroy Nineveh after all. But this did not please Jonah, 'Lord, you are being too kind. You are always ready to forgive. It's better to die than to see this.' Jonah couldn't bear to see the God of his own people being kind to foreigners. He left the city, built himself a hut and went inside.

God made a lovely tree grow to give Jonah some shade. But one day a big worm attacked the tree and killed it, so Jonah had to sit in the sun. He felt sorry for the tree; he hadn't planted it, and it had grown all by itself, but all the same, it was a shame. Then God said, 'Jonah, you are so sorry for a mere tree; why shouldn't I be sorry for a whole city of people who don't know how to find the way to happiness?'

I'm telling you stories, and you will tell them in your turn.

Between the Old Testament and the New Testament, is the turning point of the story. And it is the turning point of time, when our calendars reach zero, between BC (Before Christ) and AD (Anno Domini: in the year of Our Lord).

Who is this Jesus Christ then, that we should count the years around him in our countries?

Was he an unlucky saint? A prophet like the others in the Bible? A wise person who knew the importance of ordinary people, made the most unimportant people important, and woke those who were asleep? Was he a magic healer? Or a teacher who gave lessons? An unknown Jew, born in a stable, who spent three years with a group of twelve friends among the sick and outcasts, and then ended his life on a slave's gallows?

And how has his story come to us?

All that we know is that the first people to tell his story where the Jews who had spent three years with him. When he died they were disappointed, but fifty days later they were confidently telling the world: 'Jesus who was crucified is alive. God has raised him up. He is the Christ, the Messiah.' This was in Jerusalem around AD30.

Then the news spread. People called it 'the Good News' – that is what the word 'Gospel' means in Greek.

The books which tell about Jesus or about how Christians began and their vision of the world were written in the second half of the first century: twenty-seven books altogether.

Tell me the Bible is based on five of them: the four Gospels and the Acts of the Apostles, with a few bits from the letters of Saint Paul.

We could say, like the ending of the fourth Gospel: 'Jesus did many other signs in the presence of his disciples, which are not told in this book.'

Perhaps you're going to shrug your shoulders and say that these stories are too good to be true. Perhaps you'll swallow this book as people swallow the tales of a story-teller. Some of you may want to discuss them, while others keep them in their secret hearts the way you store up provisions for a journey.

But, you know, once you have discovered the stories of the Bible you are never the same again. Because these stories which took twenty-five generations to collect, are one of the great treasures of the human race. There's lots more for you to discover, but you already know the main thing: living with God is a great adventure for all of us.

Finally, if I tell you the Bible, it's also because you can feel someone there, just as you can feel the fresh air on your skin: there's someone there that you can trust: the God of Abraham, of Isaac and of Jacob, the God of Jesus Christ. This is a person I have met, and I want you to meet him too.

I will tell you about Jesus, and you will tell others in your turn.

The birth of Jesus, or two kings for one country

The story of the birth of Jesus
is very well known
and very surprising.
Who is this Jesus,
who makes foreigners travel,
frightens the powerful,
and is recognized by the poor?

Bethlehem was crowded with all the descendants of David who had come to the village of their ancestor to register for the census, as the Roman Emperor had commanded. Among them were Joseph a carpenter from Nazareth and his wife Mary, who was expecting a baby at any moment. The roads were packed with people and the houses were full to bursting. Joseph had to find a quiet place in the caves where the animals were stabled.

In those days wise men who studied the stars had just discovered a new star which was moving across the sky. They believed that this must mean the birth of a new king.

They left their country to follow the star and arrived at Jerusalem, where Herod the king of Judah lived. They went to the palace to ask, 'Where is the new King of the Jews? We have seen his star rising.'

Herod was worried. He was the only king of the Jews that he knew of. He sent for all his advisers and his priests to ask where a new king could be born. They told him an old passage of the Bible, 'Bethlehem, out of you shall come a leader to be the shepherd of my people Israel.'

Herod sent the wise men to Bethlehem and asked them to come to the palace on their way back to let him know, when they had seen the new baby.

Some shepherds were spending the night in the fields.

Suddenly a light surrounded them and an angel from God announced, 'Do not be frightened, here is good news of great joy for everyone. Today, in the city of David, a saviour has been born, Christ the Lord. You will find him wrapped in swaddling clothes and lying in a manger.'

The sky burst into song, 'Glory to God in the highest, and peace on earth to God's beloved people.'

The shepherds went off to see what they had been told about.

They found Mary, Joseph and the new-born baby in the manger.

It was Jesus, and the name Jesus means 'God saves'; he is also called Emmanuel which means 'God is with us'.

When they had seen him, the shepherds told the whole story of what they had seen.

Meanwhile the wise men were following the star. They arrived in their turn at the place where Jesus was. They bowed down before this child as if they were bowing before God.

Then they gave him their gifts, gold for a king, incense as an offering to God, and myrrh, the perfume used to anoint the dead. What kind of kingdom would have a king like this poor baby?

Then the wise men went back to their country without visiting Herod.

During the night Joseph had a dream; in it an angel from God warned him, 'Get up and take the baby and his mother with you and get away to Egypt. Stay there until you have further orders, because Herod is going to look for the child to kill him.' So Joseph fled to Egypt.

31

The first steps

The Gospels tell us about the anger of Herod in order to show that Jesus is a king. They tell us how the family escaped to Egypt to show us that Jesus is the new Moses. They tell us how Jesus went to the temple at the age of twelve to show that Jesus called God 'My Father' so he must be God's son.

Later, after reigning for thirty-seven years altogether, the terrible king Herod died. The angel of God appeared to Joseph in a dream, and said, 'Take the child and his mother and go back to Israel, because those who threatened his life are dead.'

Joseph, Mary and Jesus set off for Nazareth. Jesus grew up with his family and neighbours and also with God.

When he was twelve, Joseph and Mary took him on a pilgrimage to Jerusalem for the Passover; the festival lasted seven days.

Herod was clinging on to power at all costs. He sent his soldiers to Bethlehem to kill all boys less than two years old. The village sounded like a slaughterhouse, with the crying of those who were killed and their families. It was 'the massacre of the innocents'. When the killing finally stopped, the air was full of sobbing. People were crying over their children and would not be consoled because they were gone.

On the way home, after a day's journey, Joseph and Mary noticed that Jesus wasn't with their family or with friends. Worried sick, they went back to Jerusalem and spent three days looking for him; they nearly died with worry.

On the third day they found him. He was in the middle of the teachers in the great Temple of God, listening to them explaining the secrets of the Bible and discussing God's will; he was asking them questions, and explaining his thoughts about God. The teachers were amazed. His parents were very upset: Mary asked him, 'Why did you do this to us? Your father and I have been so worried.' Jesus replied, 'Why were you looking for me? Didn't you know I would be in my Father's house?'

Joseph and Mary did not understand why their child spoke about God as a child talks of his father. They kept these words in their hearts and set off all together for Nazareth.

32

The Son of God

**No more was heard of Jesus
until he was thirty.
That was when he came to be baptized,
with all those who wanted
to change their lives.
Then he went to the desert
like the people of Israel
at the time of the Exodus.**

In those days a prophet, John, was drawing the crowds and telling them, 'God is coming. Prepare the way of the Lord. Change your lives.' People came from Jerusalem, from all over Judea and from further afield. John made them go into the water of the Jordan river and baptized them.

Some of them asked each other if John was the Messiah, the Christ? John told them no, 'The person coming after me is greater than me. I'm not even worthy to undo his shoe laces. I am baptizing you with water, but he will baptize you in the Spirit of God.'

That was when Jesus arrived.

He came from Nazareth, his village in Galilee, to be baptized by John. John tried to refuse, and said, 'I ought to be baptized by you and not the other way round.' But Jesus replied, 'No, go ahead. My place is to be with you all.'

So John baptized Jesus.

And Jesus had a vision: the skies opened and the Spirit of God came to him like a bird skimming over the waters. A voice said, 'This is my beloved Son.'

Baptized by John and flooded with the Spirit of God, Jesus went off into the desert. He wanted to find out the best way to live as Son of God.

For forty days he stayed there without eating. Hunger can be a test of strength: Jesus was tested. He heard the voice of the Enemy saying, 'If you are the Son of God, turn these stones into bread.' Jesus replied, 'No. The Bible says, "People do not live by bread alone, but by the word of God." '

Being alone is a test of strength: Jesus was tested, 'If you are the Son of God, throw yourself down from the walls of Jerusalem, and God will save you; then everyone will know who you are.' Jesus replied, 'No. The Bible says, "You shall not put God to the test." '

Exhaustion is a test of strength: Jesus was tested. 'If you are the Son of God, you can rule the world, if you worship power.' Jesus replied, 'You shall worship God and nothing else.'

And Jesus who had not let these tempting dreams separate him from God, went off to tell people what kind of father God is.

The new prophet

In Galilee,
Jesus began
to tell the 'Good News':
that is what the Greek word
'Gospel' means.

When Jesus was walking on the shore of the Lake of Tiberias, he saw Simon and his brother Andrew, two fishermen, who were putting out their nets. Jesus called to them, 'Come over here. Instead of pulling your nets out of the sea, you can be pulling people towards God. I will make you fishers of men.'

A bit further on, Jesus called James and John, the two sons of Zebedee. They immediately left their father and their friends and their boat, and followed Jesus.

So Jesus now had his first disciples. He chose them to share his life and to be his witnesses of everything that happened from the beginning.

Mary, Jesus' mother, was invited to a wedding at Cana. Jesus was there too with his disciples.

The feast was going well; people were eating and drinking; the wine was flowing freely.

But by dint of hard drinking the wedding guests finished up the wine. There was nothing left; the jars were empty.

Mary warned Jesus, 'They've run out of wine.' Jesus replied, 'What do you want me to do about it? My time has not yet come.'

However, Mary went ahead and told the servants, 'Do exactly what he tells you.'

There were some very big jars there. Jesus told the servants to fill them with water, and the servants filled them up to the brim.

Jesus went on, 'Now fill a jug from them and take it to the head waiter.' The head waiter tasted it: it was wine, of the best quality. Only the servants knew what had happened. The head waiter was astonished and said to the bridegroom, 'People usually serve the best wine at the beginning; but you have kept the best for the dessert.'

This was the first time Jesus showed who he was, at Cana in Galilee. Empty glasses would have meant the end of the feast. But now the wine was flowing and the feast was back on course. The water had changed to wine, sad habit changed into new joy, shortage into plenty.

An ordinary wedding became a sign of the covenant relationship between God and people. And what happened at Cana was the first of Jesus' signs.

34

Jesus overcomes evil

This is Jesus' famous talk
called 'The Beatitudes'
because each phrase begins with
the word 'happy'
('beatus') in Latin.
But if Jesus wants everyone to be happy,
what did he do about so much evil?

The crowds came to hear words which would strengthen and challenge them, and Jesus said to them:

'Happy are those who are poor in spirit; they will share the life of God.

Happy are the kind; they will inherit the Kingdom of God.

Happy are those who weep; they will be consoled.

Happy are those who hunger and thirst for justice; they will get justice.

Happy are those who care for others; God will care for them.

Happy are those whose hearts are pure, simple and free; they shall see God.

Happy are those who know how to make peace; they shall be called "children of God".

If you are criticized, or rejected, because you follow me, be joyful; you will have a great reward in God's presence.'

One day Jesus was in a house in Capernaum, and such a large crowd had arrived to hear him that no one could get near to him.

Four men wanted to get a paralysed man to him, come what may. So they climbed the balcony and made a hole in the roof and let the sick man's stretcher down just in front of Jesus. When Jesus saw their determination and their faith he said to the paralysed man, 'Faith, friend, your sins are forgiven.'

The religious people were shocked: 'Only God can forgive sins,' they said, 'he thinks he's God.'

Jesus could feel their suspicions. So, to show that he had power to forgive, he asked them, 'Which is easier? To say to a paralysed person "Your sins are forgiven" or to say "Get up and walk"?' Then he turned to the paralysed man and said, 'Get up, take your stretcher, and go home.' So the man got up and went home in front of everybody.

One evening Jesus and his disciples were going by boat across the lake. Suddenly a great storm broke out. The lake went wild. The boat was lifted up on the crest of the waves and then plunged down into deep troughs.

Jesus was in the back of the boat sleeping peacefully. His friends woke him up, 'Master, we're going to drown. Don't you care?' Jesus shook his fist at the wind. He commanded the storm, 'Silence. Be still.'

The waves which were going to sink the passengers into a watery grave, calmed down and cradled the boat again. Jesus said to his friends, 'Why were you frightened? Have you no faith in God? Haven't you any faith in me?'

The apostles felt better, but were still puzzled, and asked each other, 'Who is this, that even the winds obey him and storms cannot stop him sleeping? He has no fear of destructive winds, nor of being swamped by the tide of evil. Who is he then, this Jesus?'

35

The face of God

**Everybody had heard of Jesus,
but people wanted to know
who he really was.
Jesus asked them about this,
but what was the answer?
And who knew how to answer?**

Jesus and his disciples arrived in the north of the province of Galilee around the source of the river Jordan. There Jesus asked them, 'What are people saying about me?' His disciples answered, 'Some have got you confused with John the Baptist. Others think you are a great prophet of God.' Jesus went on, 'But what about you?' Peter answered, 'You are the Christ, the Son of the Living God.' Jesus praised him, 'You need to know how lucky you are, Peter, because no one can find this out all alone. God must have told you this. I will call you Peter because it means "Rock" and you are the rock on which all who believe in my name can rely.'

Jesus asked them to keep Peter's reply to themselves. And he went on to tell them for the first time how he would have to suffer greatly and be put to death, and that he would rise again. Peter was horrified, 'God forbid,' he said, 'the Christ, the one sent by God, can't possibly die.' Jesus told him he was wrong, 'This time what you say doesn't come from God. Instead of blocking my path, you should be following me.'

Six days later Jesus took Peter, James and John up a high mountain. Suddenly the three men were astonished: Jesus seemed to be glowing with light; his clothes were all white and shining. They thought they saw the great prophet Elijah with him and Moses, who had received the Ten Commandments of the Covenant. Peter wanted to make this wonderful moment last. He said to Jesus, 'This is a happy moment. I'm going to build three huts, one for you, one for Moses and one for Elijah.'

But suddenly Peter, James and John felt themselves surrounded by a strange luminous cloud and they heard a voice saying, 'This is my beloved Son. Listen to him.' They threw themselves down on the ground, trembling. They shuddered, overpowered by the holiness of what was happening.

But Jesus came to them and touched them and said, 'Up you get, don't be afraid.' When they looked up, the three apostles could not see anyone else there, except Jesus with his usual expression. And as they went down the mountain Jesus told them not to tell anyone about what they had seen and heard until after his resurrection.

———

Who is Jesus? Peter gave a good answer to this question, because he was inspired by God. On the mountain it was even more clear that Peter had given the right answer; this answer was confirmed by God himself: Jesus is God's Son. But in that case why did Jesus tell Peter and his friends to keep the secret? Because it is not enough to know the right answer. They would have to learn to recognize the face of God not just in Jesus when he was glowing with light, but also, later, in Jesus twisted on the cross.

36

The secret of prayer

The great secret of Jesus' life
was his friendship with God
his father: a father he could
always turn to in trust.
Jesus invites us to share
his secret by praying.

Jesus used to say, 'When you pray, don't be like
the "look at me" people who say their prayers in
public to impress people. Go into your room and
shut the door, and speak to God in secret. Prayer
is not something flashy which you have to display
to get God's attention. Do not keep on repeating
the same words. God is not going to be persuaded
by the number of words you use. But do not be
afraid to speak to God. Knock on his door
whenever you want . . . Here's a story:

*Once there was a villager who went in the
middle of the night to knock on his neighbour's
door:*
"Neighbour, lend me three rolls.
*One of my friends has come to stay and I have
nothing to give him to eat."*
*The neighbour got up and wanted to shut him
up:*
"Shush. Let me sleep. You'll wake the children."

*But the man insisted: he wouldn't give in. So,
whether out of kindness, or in order to get rid of
him, the neighbour ended up giving him what he
needed.'*
Jesus finished, 'If your neighbour will put
himself out in this way, surely God is even more
likely to hear what you ask for. God knows what
you need.'

Among those who were listening to Jesus were some religious people who took their prayers very seriously and were convinced that they were good believers. Jesus told another story:

'Once there were two men who went into the temple to pray.

The first was a religious Pharisee, and he stood and prayed, "My God I honour you. I do not steal, and I'm never unfaithful to my wife. I fast twice a week and I pay my contributions to the temple." When he saw the other man he added, "Thank you, God, that I am not like this pathetic tax collector." Meanwhile the tax collector didn't dare even look upwards, and said, "O God have mercy on me. I'm so far from what I ought to be."

And Jesus added, 'Well then, I'm telling you, God heard the prayer of this man and regarded him as a saint. But God could do nothing for the Pharisee because he thought he could become a saint by his own efforts.'

Then a disciple interrupted Jesus and said, 'Lord, teach us to pray.' Jesus replied, 'This is the way we pray: Our Father in heaven, hallowed be your name. May your Kingdom come, and your will be done on earth, as it is in heaven. Give us this day our daily bread, and forgive us our offences, as we forgive those who offend us. Do not put us to the test.'

———

Since then, the 'Our Father' is the prayer of all baptized Christians.

81

37

The secret of brotherhood and sisterhood

**The great secret of Jesus' life
is his closeness to God
his Father:
a father who is
the father of all human beings.
Jesus invites us
to share his secret
living as brothers and sisters.**

Someone asked Jesus, 'Tell us what will happen at the end of the world.'

Jesus replied, 'The king will be sitting on his throne. He will sort the people out, some on the right, some on the left, as the shepherd separates the sheep from the goats.

Then the king will say to those on his right, "Come, the beloved of my Father, come into the Kingdom. When I was hungry you fed me; and when I was thirsty you gave me something to drink; I was a stranger and you welcomed me; I was sick and you visited me." These people will ask, "When did we see you like that? When did we do all these things?"

The king will reply, "Every time you did anything for the smallest or most unfortunate people, you did it for me."

Then he will turn to his left and say, "Go away, you are condemned. For when I was hungry you gave me nothing to eat; I was naked and you gave me no clothes. I was in prison and you did not help me." They also will ask, "When did we see you hungry, or naked, or in prison?" He will reply, "Every time you did not do this for the smallest or the most unfortunate person, you did not do it for me." '

When Jesus had finished speaking, the disciples realized that the king of the Kingdom of God was Jesus, and that he really regarded the unfortunate as his brothers and sisters.

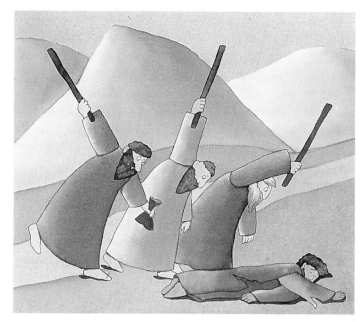

A scripture scholar interrupted Jesus, 'God's law commands us, "You shall love God with all your heart and your neighbour as yourself." But who is my neighbour? Who is it I must love?' In reply Jesus told this story:

'A man was going from Jerusalem to Jericho and was attacked by bandits. They robbed him and left him for dead. The first person to arrive was a priest, who went by without stopping. Then came someone who worked at the temple of God; he also left the wounded man alone. Then came a Samaritan, who did not do much about his religion. When he saw the wounded man, he was concerned. He went up to him, cleaned and bandaged his wounds. Then he put him on his own donkey, and took him to a hotel, and paid the hotel-keeper to look after the wounded man.'

Then Jesus asked the questioner: 'In your view, which of the three passers-by was a neighbour to the injured man? Who showed love?' The questioner replied, 'The third one, the one who took care of him.'

When they had heard this story all those present realized that Jesus was asking them to be like himself in future, a neighbour or brother to everyone.

38

The secret of being lost and found

**The great secret of Jesus' life
is his closeness to God
his Father:
a father who is so happy
to find what is lost,
those who feel they have lost their way.
Jesus invites us
to let him find us
and share his secret.**

Jesus was invited to the house of Simon, one of the Pharisees who usually rejected Jesus. The meal began. Suddenly a woman came in and threw herself weeping at Jesus' feet; she kissed his feet and poured perfume on them. For Simon this proved that Jesus was not the prophet he claimed to be. Otherwise he would have known that this woman was unfortunate, a lost woman, and he would have kept her at arm's length. Jesus did not stop her, and told this story:

'Once there was a banker. One of his customers owed him six hundred silver pieces, and another owed fifty. He cancelled their debts. Which of the two will love him more?'

Simon replied, 'The one who owed him more.' Jesus answered, 'Well said. And now you see, this woman believes that she owes a large debt, and she has never stopped covering me with kisses, while you didn't even kiss me when I arrived. As her heart is overflowing with love, she knows she is forgiven. And as she knows she is forgiven, her heart overflows with love.'

Then Jesus said to the woman, 'Your sins are forgiven. Go in peace.'

The other guests were amazed. They asked each other, 'Who is this Jesus, who is not embarrassed when a lost woman clings to his feet; who sees in this only a gesture of love and even goes on to forgive sins?'

Another time, Jesus was again with people who were not very respectable. Some people who thought well of themselves muttered about this, 'What is he doing with those people? They're lost anyway.' So Jesus told another story:

'Once there was a poor woman who had ten silver coins. One day she could only find nine. So she got a lamp to light up the dark corners of the house and searched everywhere, turned everything over, turned the house upside down. In

the end she found the lost coin. Then with great joy she called her friends and neighbours: "Come and rejoice with me, for I have found the coin I had lost." '

And Jesus went on, 'This is how God rejoices when someone who has been lost is found.'

Jesus' way of presenting God was certainly unexpected: God is not like the people who thought well of themselves; God never gives up anyone as a lost cause.

39

The protector of children

**The gospels also tell us
about Jesus' griefs and struggles.
Children often
count for nothing.
Jesus is fighting to show
that the Kingdom of God is
open to children.**

When a stranger arrives in a village the children run to meet him. They are always the first to come out to see. When Jesus came towards a village the children clung on to his arms like bunches of grapes hanging from a vine. They were told off by the grown ups, who thought that Jesus didn't have time to waste with the children. But Jesus used to say, 'Let the children come to me. The Kingdom of God is a present for the children, and for other people like them.'

In this way he asked everyone to discover the child in herself or himself so as to be able to welcome God.

A bit later, Jesus came to Jericho. People crowded to see him pass. Zacchaeus the tax collector was too short to see over people's heads. So he climbed up a big sycamore tree, and from up there he could see Jesus. Jesus arrived under the tree and looked up at Zacchaeus and said, 'Zacchaeus, come down from your tree. I want to go to your house today.'

Zacchaeus jumped down quickly. He ran home quickly to welcome Jesus. When people saw this they complained, 'Jesus is going too far. Now he's

going to a thief's house. Zacchaeus isn't worthy to entertain Jesus in his house.' Zacchaeus himself was overjoyed; he promised Jesus, 'I've made a lot of money. So, Lord, I'm going to give half of my wealth to the poor. And I know there are lots of people I've cheated: I'll give them back four times as much as I took from them.'

Jesus said, 'Today, salvation has come to this house. Zacchaeus is also part of the people of God. And I have come to search for those who are lost.'

40

Jesus fights on God's side

God is often criticized,
misunderstood, dishonoured,
unloved and even accused.
Jesus fights the religious leaders
and the wrong ideas they have about God.
He takes up God's defence:
God is not an accountant,
nor resentful, nor a master to be served,
God is a father.

out the dove-sellers, sheep-sellers and bull-sellers. He thundered, 'Take all that stuff away, do not turn my father's house into a market.'

Some of the Jews came to ask him, 'What right do you have to do this?'

Jesus replied, 'Are you asking me to prove my right by a sign? Destroy the temple and in three days I will build it up again.'

When he said this, Jesus was talking about himself, and how he would be killed and would rise again on the third day. Jesus is the living temple, God with us.

As he was leaving the temple, Jesus saw a man who had been blind from birth. His disciples believed that God had sent the blindness as a

Jesus, the Jew from Nazareth, joined the other pilgrims coming up to the temple in Jerusalem for the Passover. There was a huge crowd. The leaders were telling the stories of the Jewish people and Moses, when God saved them from slavery in Egypt. They said that God would keep the promise to save them again. The priests were preparing the ceremonies, and the animal sellers were waiting for the pilgrims to come and buy their animals for sacrificing.

But when Jesus arrived he got angry and overturned the money-changer's tables. He drove

punishment. They asked, 'Master, is it this man's fault, or his parents? What did they do to deserve this?'

Jesus defended God, 'God is not there to punish,

and no one is guilty. You shall see what God can do.' Then he spat on the ground and made mud with the saliva. Then he put this mud on the eyes of the blind man and sent him to wash in the pool of Siloam. When the blind man came back he could see perfectly.

The people asked, 'Is this really the blind man who used to beg?' The blind man, who was cured now, replied, 'Yes, it's really me. Jesus put mud on my eyes and now I can see.'

The Pharisees could not agree amongst themselves. Some said, 'It's the seventh day of the week, the day of rest; the Law says people should not work or care for people on this day. Jesus is not keeping the Law; he's way out of line.' Others replied, 'If God was not with him, he would not be able to do this.'

Then they asked the man who had been blind, 'What do you think about him?' The man replied, 'He's a prophet.'

The Jews didn't believe what they were seeing, so they sent for the man's parents. The parents swore that this was really their son, and that he had always been blind. Then the blind man had more to say, 'Now I can see clearly,' he said. 'If Jesus did not come from God he would not be able to do such things. I don't know why you can't see this.'

Blinded by their anger, the Pharisees threw him out.

When Jesus heard this he went to see the man, 'Do you believe in the Messiah who comes from God?' he asked. The man said, 'Who is he?' Jesus replied, 'You can see him.' Then the man who had been miraculously healed said, 'I believe.' And Jesus added, 'I have come to make the blind see, and to show up the blindness of those who think they can see everything.'

41

Jesus fights for life against death

Jesus had fought with the scorn of important people, the jealousy of the Pharisees who thought they were the experts on God; now he has to face the last enemy: death.

brother will rise to life again.'

Martha well knew that her religion taught that this was possible, but she was not consoled.

So Jesus went on to say, 'I am the resurrection and I am life. Whoever believes in me, even though he dies, shall live. Do you believe this?' And Martha said, 'Yes, Lord, I believe that you are the Christ, the Son of God, who was to come into the world.'

Martha went to tell Mary that Jesus had arrived. Mary came out of the house with her friends, and they all went to Lazarus' tomb. Mary was sobbing.

Jesus continued on his journey and the disciples followed him, as if they were following a trail. Suddenly a man rushed up and said, 'Lord, your friend Lazarus, from Bethany, is sick. His sisters Martha and Mary have sent me to find you.'

Jesus gave a strange answer; he said, 'This sickness will show people the glory of God', and he stayed where he was for two more days.

When Jesus and his disciples finally arrived at Bethany, Lazarus had been dead and buried for four days. Martha and Mary were wrapped up in their grief. But when they heard Jesus had arrived Martha got up and went to meet him. She said to him, 'If you had only been here my brother would not have died. But even so, I know you can ask God for anything.' Jesus replied, 'Your

Jesus was very moved and distressed; he wept, with death in his heart. People saw this and said, 'Look how much he loved Lazarus.' Others mocked and said, 'If he could open the eyes of the blind, then he could have stopped this man from dying.'

Then Jesus asked them to roll away the stone from the tomb, and then he prayed to God, 'Father, thank you for having heard my prayer. I know well that you hear everything I ask. I am saying this so that the people around me may know that you have sent me.' Then he shouted in a loud voice, 'Lazarus, get up, come out.' Death was overcome and Lazarus came out of the tomb. Many of those who were there and saw Lazarus alive, started to believe in Jesus. They were full of joy, ready to take up a new life. The important people, though, were annoyed and said, 'If we let Jesus go on like this, everybody will believe in him and we shall be out of a job. Something will have to be done to put a stop to this.'

So the day when Jesus brought Lazarus back to life, was the day his enemies decided he should die.

42

Jesus enters Jerusalem and shares a farewell meal with his friends

This is the heart of the story of Jesus:
four events which each gospel
tells at length,
each in its own way,
like holy words.

The feast of the Passover was getting near and large crowds had come to Jerusalem; the city was noisy and overcrowded. Then people heard that Jesus was coming and they went out to line the route. When they saw him, riding a young donkey, they shouted, 'Blessed is he who comes in the name of the Lord! Hosanna in the highest!'

As if they were welcoming a king, they spread their coats on the road.

The religious leaders frowned, because they could remember the words of the prophet Zechariah, 'Jerusalem, your King Christ is coming, a king riding simply on a young donkey.' They said to each other, 'Jesus thinks he is the Christ of God, and everyone is on his side. This has got out of hand.' Then Judas, one of Jesus' twelve apostles, plotted with the priests to hand Jesus over to them.

A few days later, Jesus met with his apostles for supper: there was an atmosphere of Passover that night. The Jews were celebrating, as they did every year, the passing over of God in Egypt when God came to set them free. However, something unexpected happened. While they were eating Jesus said, 'One of you is going to betray me.' They were very distressed, and

started asking him one by one, 'Is it me?' When Judas' turn came, Jesus replied, 'You said it.' And Judas went out into the night.

Then Jesus took the bread and blessed it, broke it and shared it with his friends, saying, 'Take and eat. This is my body.' He took the cup of wine, thanked God and said, 'Drink this all of you. This is my blood, the blood of the new covenant. Do this in remembrance of me.'

Then Jesus added, 'One day, everyone will be invited to the great feast of the Lord, and I shall drink with you the new wine in the Kingdom of God.'

After supper, Jesus and his disciples sang some hymns, the traditional psalms of the Passover. They had decided to go to the Mount of Olives, which was opposite the city gate. They were just setting off when Jesus said, 'Tonight, because of me, you will be shocked and you will be put to the test.'

Peter spoke, 'Even if everyone gives up because of you, I shall never give up.' Jesus replied, 'This very night, before the cock crows, you will deny me three times.'

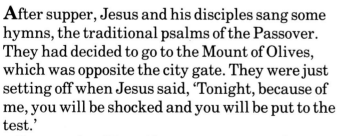

43

The arrest and trial

After his triumphant entry into Jerusalem and his farewell supper, Jesus had to face injustice all alone. He was denied, abandoned by his friends and it seemed as if God had abandoned him too. Even though Jesus was God, he still had to cope with everything that could happen to a human being.

Jesus was dying of grief. He asked Peter, James and John to stay with him. But the three friends fell asleep. Jesus prayed, 'My God, my father, if it's possible, keep me safe and don't let me suffer . . . but may your will be done.' He looked round at the three men, who were lying under the olive trees. They hadn't been able to stay awake. They were asleep and he was alone in the night.

Even God seemed to have abandoned him. Jesus was desperate. He begged, 'God, I'm lost. I'm sick with fear. I'm desperate. I want to live, and I have to die. God, my father, I give you my life; I put it in your hands.'

Then Jesus woke Peter up, 'Peter, couldn't you even stay awake for one hour? Now, it's done. Those who want my death are coming.'

They heard footsteps in the dark. A company of armed soldiers was coming towards the garden. They were led by Judas, though he was one of Jesus' friends; he would be the one to point Jesus out. Judas came up to Jesus and greeted him, calling him 'Master', and kissed him. That was the signal. The soldiers arrested Jesus, and he did not fight back or defend himself. He was arrested and led away like a bandit in front of his disciples who were terrified.

They took Jesus to the religious court, where the priests, the elders and the scribes who were experts in the Law were assembled. The questioning began. They accused him of so many things, 'I heard him claiming that he could destroy the temple of God and build it again in three days.' They were provoking him, but he stayed silent. The High Priest finally asked him, 'Are you the Christ, the Son of God, yes or no?' Jesus replied, 'You have said it. From now on I shall be with God. The Lord will overcome my enemies.' At these words the High Priest lost his temper: 'That's enough,' he cried, 'this man has no respect for God, he's a blasphemer. He deserves to die.'

Meanwhile Peter was warming himself in the yard with the guards and servants. A maid recognized him by the firelight, and said, 'Aren't you a disciple of Jesus?' Peter denied it. Another maid said, 'Yes, you are one of his people.' Peter denied again, 'No, I'm not one of his people.' A third person said, 'Yes, you were with Jesus. And you've got the same accent as he has.' The third time Peter denied it, 'I don't know the man.' At that moment the cock crew.

Peter had denied Jesus to save his life, though he loved him. He wept. Judas had died of shame: he had no hope and no friends left. He went and hanged himself.

Jesus, meanwhile, was sent by the High Priest to Pontius Pilate, the Roman Governor, because only the Romans had the power to put people to death. This was an evil night . . .

95

44

Death on the cross

The religious leaders had found Jesus guilty. Now it was the turn of the state authorities. Jesus was an innocent martyr. But if he was God, then God was dying on the cross.

The High Priests took Jesus to Pilate, and accused him, 'Jesus is a trouble-maker. He attracts crowds and tells them not to pay taxes to Rome. He claims he is a king.' Pilate questioned Jesus, 'Are you the King of the Jews?' Jesus replied, 'Those are your words, not mine.' Pilate turned to the High Priests, 'I cannot see that he is guilty of anything, but I'll have your King of the Jews beaten.' He hoped this would satisfy them. But the crowd was excited and howled all the more. So Pilate made another suggestion, 'I have two prisoners, Jesus and Barabbas. In honour of the Passover festival I'll set one free for you. You can choose which one.' A deafening cry went up, 'Barabbas! Barabbas!'

Pilate went on, 'Then what shall I do with Jesus?' The crowd shouted, 'Death! Death!' The situation was turning into a riot. When he saw that he could not talk them out of it, Pilate condemned Jesus. But publicly he washed his hands, as he did not want to be responsible for Jesus' death: he washed his hands of it.

Then he released Barabbas and handed Jesus over to the soldiers, who mocked him. They put a king's robe on him, and a crown of thorns on his head, and bowed down in front of him saying: 'Hail, King of the Jews.'

Then they took Jesus to the 'place of the skull' (which is called 'Golgotha' in Hebrew and 'Calvary' in Latin).

Jesus was crucified together with two robbers. When he saw his enemies he prayed, 'Father, forgive them; they don't know what they are doing.' People laughed at him, saying, 'He saved others, but he can't save himself.' One of the robbers insulted him too. But the other whispered, 'Lord, remember me when you come into your Kingdom.' Jesus promised him, 'Today you will be with me in Paradise.'

Jesus saw Mary his mother, and his disciple John near the cross. He asked them to look after each other. He said to his mother, 'Woman, here is your son.' And to John, 'Here is your mother.'

Then he shouted, 'My God, my God, why have you forsaken me?' It was almost midday, but in spite of that it was darker than it has ever been in daytime. Finally he gave a loud cry, 'Father, I put my life in your hands.' And he died.

When the Roman guard saw what was happening he said, 'Truly this Jesus is a good and holy man.'

Then a man from Arimathea, called Joseph, arrived. He had got permission from Pilate to bury Jesus. He took him down from the cross, wrapped his body in a sheet and put it in a tomb cut out of the rock, and shut the door with a huge block of stone. Night fell like a curtain.

45

Witnesses of the resurrection

**God has experienced everything
that can happen to a human being.
Jesus died and was buried.
However,
that was not the end of the story ...
Do we go through
everything God goes through?**

Two nights had passed since Jesus' death. It was dawn on the third day, and day was just taking over from night. Mary Magdalene arrived at Jesus' tomb and found it wide open. The stone which had sealed it had been rolled aside.

She immediately ran off to tell Peter, 'They've taken the Lord out of the tomb and we don't know where they have put him.'

Peter and John rushed to see. Peter went into the tomb first. He found the cloths which had been wrapped round Jesus on the ground, and the sheet, still folded, lying separately.

When John saw this he realized that Jesus was no longer lying dead. The two disciples went off again.

But Mary Magdalene was crying outside the tomb. Then she saw two angels sitting on the stone bench beside where Jesus' body had been lying. They asked her, 'Woman, why are you crying?' Mary Magdalene replied, 'Because they have taken away my Lord and I don't know where they have put him.'

She turned round. There was Jesus standing in front of her. She was looking at him but didn't recognize him.

Jesus said to her, 'Woman, why are you crying? Who are you looking for?' She thought he must be the gardener and she asked him, 'Tell me where you have put the body. I will go and get it.' Jesus said, 'Mary'. Then she recognized him, 'Master'. Jesus went on, 'Don't hold on to me. But go and find my brothers and tell them: I am going to my father, who is your father too; to my God, who is your God too.'

Mary Magdalene ran off to spread the good news, 'I've seen the Lord alive.'

The evening of the same day, the disciples were in the house. They had locked the doors for fear of attack. Suddenly Jesus was there in the middle of them. He reassured them, 'Peace be with you.' And so that they should not think he was a ghost, he showed them his scars, his torn hands, the traces of his wounds. Then he said again, 'Peace be with you.'

They were so happy. They felt the breath of Jesus' life and they began to liven up themselves. This is like the story of Creation when God's breath gave life to Adam.

Thomas wasn't there at the time; he came in after Jesus had gone and the others said to him, 'We've seen the Lord.' Thomas thought they were dreaming. 'I'll believe it when I see the nail marks on his hands,' he said. A week later everyone was together again and Jesus again appeared among them. He held his hands out to

Thomas and said, 'Put your fingers in the marks. Start believing.' Thomas said, 'My Lord and my God.' Then Jesus went on, 'You believe because you have seen. Happy are those who believe without having seen.'

46

A new breath

**After the Gospels
we come to a new book of the Bible:
the Acts of the Apostles.
Just as Jesus was
the hero of the Gospels,
so the main hero of the Acts
is the Spirit of God, who helps
the little group of disciples to grow.**

Jesus' apostles, his mother, and all the other disciples were together in Jerusalem. A new apostle, Matthias, had taken Judas' place. He had followed Jesus before his death, and had seen him risen, so he could be an accepted witness.

They prayed behind locked doors; they told each other the stories of the wedding at Cana, the stilling of the storm, the meeting with Zacchaeus. They reminded each other of the words of Jesus. It was as if Jesus was still there talking with them.

They shared meals in the way Jesus had asked them to during his last supper with them. It was as if Jesus was still there feeding them.

The group met regularly. They believed that Jesus was still calling them to meet, and they felt that he was there among them.

On the day of Pentecost they were all together. Suddenly there was a great noise like a violent gust of wind. The house was full of it. A glowing cloud surrounded them and it was as if they were handing each other tongues of fire, which settled on each of them.

The people who had come to Jerusalem for the feast from all corners of the world, rushed to see what was happening. They found Jesus' disciples outside, full of joy, and each heard them speaking in his or her own language.

Everyone was astonished. Some were speechless, others said, 'They're drunk.'

Then Peter spoke, 'No, we aren't drunk. Anyway it's only nine in the morning. What has happened today was promised by the prophet Joel in the Bible, "One day God will pour out the Holy Spirit on us; our sons and daughters will be prophets."

You remember Jesus of Nazareth, who healed the man who was blind from birth, the paralysed man in Capernaum and many others. You killed him, you made the Romans crucify him. Well, this same Jesus has been raised to life by God, and we are his witnesses. He is alive with God.

He is the Messiah we were waiting for. And it's he who has sent the breath of God to us, and put the Spirit of God in us.

God has made him Lord.'

A lot of those who listened were overwhelmed by what had happened, and convinced by Peter's sermon, and wanted to become disciples of Jesus. More than three thousand people asked to be baptized in the name of Jesus Christ.

This is how God's promise to Abraham to be on his side for ever, was passed on to these people from Jerusalem and from other places, to their children and grandchildren.

47

New Christians

**To begin with
Christians used to meet
in their houses.
The word 'church' means 'meeting'
in Greek.
That's why a meeting of Christians
is called the Church.**

In the first Church in Jerusalem all the crowds of people who had become Jesus' disciples were as one. They shared everything. Those who owned lands or houses sold them and shared the money with everyone, according to need.

The first Christians were all Jews. But some of them who didn't come from Jerusalem and only spoke Greek, felt left out.

So to avoid arguments between the two groups seven people were chosen to work with the Greek-speaking Jewish Christians: Stephen, Philip, Prochorus, Nicanor, Timon, Parmenas and Nicolas. Peter laid his hands on their heads and the whole Church prayed for them. They were called 'deacons' which means 'people who serve others'.

One day a group of people accused Stephen of criticizing Moses and of saying that God did not live in the temple in Jerusalem. They took him to the High Priest's court. Everyone was watching Stephen, as if he was an angel. The High Priest asked him, 'Did you in fact say "Jesus of Nazareth will destroy the Temple and change the Law of God which Moses gave us?" ' Stephen did not let them make him nervous. He knew the Bible by heart. He reminded them of the stories of Abraham, Isaac and Jacob, of Joseph and Moses. Full of God's power he said, 'You are hard-hearted. Jesus is the Messiah, the Christ whom the prophets promised us in the Bible: that is Jesus.' His words made the priests very angry.

The judges were so angry they could not take any more. They dragged Stephen out of the city and hurled rocks at him as hard as they could, to kill him. Before he died Stephen just managed to pray, 'Lord Jesus, I put my life in your hands. Lord Jesus, forgive them.' Then, torn to pieces by the hail of rocks he died right in front of Paul, one of the most dangerous enemies of the Christians.

Philip, one of the seven deacons, was on the way from Jerusalem to Gaza when he met a chariot. The driver was a foreigner, the Chancellor of the Exchequer to the Queen of Ethiopia.

In his chariot, this Ethiopian was reading aloud a passage from the book of the prophet Isaiah. Philip asked him, 'Do you understand what you are reading?' The foreigner said, 'No, I need someone to explain it to me. Come and read it with me and sit beside me.' So Philip showed the Ethiopian how the ancient prophecies in the Bible, and all the promises of God, came true in Jesus Christ. The Ethiopian broke in, 'Look, there is water. Why shouldn't I be baptized and be a disciple of Jesus Christ myself?' Philip asked

him, 'Do you believe with all your heart that Jesus was sent by God?' The Ethiopian replied, 'Yes, I believe that Jesus is the Christ, the Son of God, sent to us all.' Then Philip baptized the foreigner.

Meanwhile Peter had baptized Cornelius, an officer in the Roman army, and all his family. Up to that time the first Christians had all been Jews by birth or by adoption. From that time on, it was no longer necessary to be a Jew in order to be a disciple of Jesus Christ. Peter announced that God invited everyone without exception, and that Jesus had come for the sake of every nation on earth.

The group of Christians went on growing.

48

A new apostle

His Jewish name was Saul,
his Greek name was Paul.
He was a Roman citizen; he knew Greek;
he was a Jewish Pharisee.
Because of his beliefs
he had supported the stoning of Stephen
and he persecuted Christians.
However, we now call him
Saint Paul . . .

In those days the Christians of Jerusalem were persecuted. Paul would go into their houses and drag out men and women and throw them into prison. The survivors left the city to live in other places. So Paul in his hatred decided to go after them. He got letters of recommendation from the High Priest which gave him the right to go to the city of Damascus and get rid of the disciples of Jesus there.

On the Damascus road, towards midday, as Paul approached the city, a blinding light suddenly fell from the sky and surrounded him. He was knocked to the ground and heard a voice, 'Paul, Paul, why do you persecute me?' Paul asked, 'Who are you?' And then he heard, 'I am Jesus, and you are persecuting me. Now get up and go into the city. There you will be told what you must do.' Paul got up but he was completely blind. His fellow-travellers were amazed, and led him by the hand into Damascus.

They went to stay with someone called Judas in Straight Street. Paul spent three days in the dark, neither eating nor drinking, completely overcome. At that time there was in Damascus a Jew who had become a Christian, called Ananias. Ananias knew that Paul had come from Jerusalem to arrest the Christians of Damascus. But as a result of a vision he went to visit Paul, 'Brother Paul,' he said, 'Jesus has sent me to you. It was Jesus who appeared to you on the Damascus road so that you can stop being blind and be filled with his Spirit.' Then Ananias put his hands on Paul, and at once Paul could see again. Ananias told him, 'The God of our fathers has chosen you to spread the word about him and to witness to him before everyone, Jews and Gentiles.'

And Paul was baptized. From then on he was a Christian.

He gradually recovered his strength, and then he went to preach in the synagogues, 'Jesus is the Son of God. He is the Messiah.' Those who heard him were most surprised, 'Is this the same person who was fanatically against Christians?' they wondered. Paul grew in confidence and became more and more important. Eventually some leading citizens decided he must be arrested. They put a guard on all the city gates day and night. But Paul had been told about the plan.

One night his friends hid him in a basket and let him the whole way down the city walls from a window which overlooked them.

Paul was rescued, and he was able to get away. This was just the beginning of his adventures.

New communities

Three years after his baptism Paul met the apostles in Jerusalem. They were pleased at his conversion, and sent him to visit the Church in Antioch. That is where the disciples of Jesus were first called 'Christians'. The Church was really being launched into the world at large.

The Christians of Antioch sent Paul out as a missionary. He went to Cyprus and then to Perga in Pamphilia.

In each place Paul first went to find the Jews to tell them that Jesus was the Lord, the Messiah of God whom they were expecting. But often he was rejected. Then he turned to the Gentiles, the people who had other religions.

One day Paul landed in Athens, a Greek city with many temples to all sorts of gods and goddesses. The Athenians were always interested in anything new, so they listened to Paul: he said, 'Athenians, I can see a monument with the inscription "To the Unknown God". This is the God whom you worship without knowing, the creator of heaven and earth. God is the giver of life, and we are God's family. God is not made of gold or marble, not made by humans. God is alive.' As the Athenians were interested, Paul went on: 'This God has brought someone to life from death: Jesus.' As soon as they heard the words 'brought to life' the Athenians started to laugh at him. They refused to believe. This was a failure and Paul had to go on somewhere else.

Paul went to Corinth, a town of sailors and merchants. There he met the disciples of Jesus in the 'Christians' house'. Aquila was there and his wife Priscilla, Stephanas and all his family, and Phoebe who was the leader of the Christians in the port. There were skilled workers there, slaves, and better-off people. There was such a variety of people that they found it difficult to get on with each other, even during the Eucharist. So Paul said to them, 'A body has feet, hands, ears, eyes, a nose and a head . . . Imagine the foot saying to the hand, "I'm not a hand, so I'm not part of the body". Imagine the eye saying to the hand, "I don't need you." And what if the whole

body was a big ear, how would it smell? Each member is necessary to the body: and you are the body of Christ.'

Paul set off again, this time to Antioch, and then on to Ephesus, Troas, Miletus and finally Jerusalem. But when he got there he was arrested by the Romans because some people in Asia had complained about him, saying, 'This man is an enemy of the Jewish people: he claims that Jesus, whom he calls Christ, came for the whole world, for the Gentiles as much as for the Jews, who were specially chosen by God to make himself known.'

Paul defended himself and said, 'I am a Jew myself; I studied in Jerusalem, under Gamaliel. All the Jews here know me. I used to fight the Christians as you do. But on the road to Damascus Jesus of Nazareth called me. From then on I became his witness before the whole world, and especially the Gentiles.'

When he said this the accusers shouted, 'This individual must be got rid of.' Paul was condemned and put in prison. But because he had been born at Tarsus, a city of the Roman Empire, he was a Roman citizen and he had the right to appeal to the Roman Emperor himself. He did appeal, and was put on a ship to go to Rome, the capital of the empire. It was a long voyage and the stormy season was beginning. A huge storm broke out, the ship sprang a leak and was wrecked on the island of Malta.

Three months later Paul finally arrived in Rome and took advantage of the opportunity to tell everyone who visited him about Jesus Christ. 'Brothers and sisters,' he used to say, 'whether you are descendants of Abraham or not, this good news is for you: when God raised Jesus from the dead, he was faithful to the promise. Through Jesus all the people of the earth can know God.'

A few years later, in AD63, Paul died in Rome as a martyr; he was beheaded. He had dictated letters to his secretary, to all the Christian communities he had founded, all around the Aegean sea. That is how the good news of Jesus Christ, which Paul preached, reached us. And the Gospel of God goes on spreading, day after day.

CONTENTS

The books of the Bible where these stories can be found

Genesis (for pages 8 to 39), Exodus (pages 40 to 51), Numbers (pages 46 to 51), Deuteronomy (pages 50 to 51), Joshua (pages 52 to 53), Judges (pages 54 to 55), Samuel 1 and 2 (pages 56 to 59), Daniel, 2 Chronicles, Ezra (pages 60 to 61), Judith (pages 62 to 63), Jonah (pages 64 to 65). Gospels of Matthew, Mark, Luke and John (pages 68 to 99), Acts of the Apostles (pages 100 to 107), 1 Corinthians (pages 106 to 107).